CONSENSUS

CONSENSUS

A LIBERAL LOOKS AT HIS PARTY

ROY MACLAREN

MOSAIC PRESS
OAKVILLE   NEW YORK   LONDON

Canadian Cataloguing in Publication Data

MacLaren, Roy, 1934 –
    Consensus : a Liberal looks at his party

ISBN : 0-88962-271-x paper

1. Liberal Party of Canada
I. Title

JL197.L5M24 1984   324.27106 C84-099415-x

Published by Mosaic Press, P.O. Box 1032, Oakville, Ontario, L6J 5E9, Canada.

Published with the assistance of the Canada Council and the Ontario Arts Council.

Typeset by Belbin & Miners Typography Ltd.
Design by Doug Frank.
Printed and bound in Canada.
Cover design by Steve Manley
Cover Photo by: Sandy Gage
ISBN 0-88962-271-x paper

Distributed in the United States by Flatiron Books, 175 Fifth Avenue, Suite 814, New York, N.Y. 10010, U.S.A.

Distributed in the U.K. by John Calder (Publishers) Ltd., 18 Brewer Street, London, W1R 4AS, England.

Distributed in New Zealand and Australia by Pilgrims South Press, P.O. Box 5101, Dunedin, New Zealand.

CONTENTS

PREFACE

When I was a small child in Vancouver, my father lifted me on his shoulders to see King George VI, Queen Elizabeth and Mackenzie King pass along Kitsilano Beach in an open black automobile to the somewhat self-conscious cheers of a few spectators. My four-year-old eyes were for the King and Queen. But my father made certain that I also noted the presence of the Prime Minister. He seemed pink and plump, sitting rather nervously, this leader who, unbeknownst to us, would rightly describe himself in his diary as "a little fat round man" with "no expression of lofty character."

Was that really *the* Prime Minister of Canada, *the* Mackenzie King from distant Ottawa, about whom adults seemed to have such violent feelings pro or con? Looking back now I would add: was this the man who had such a reputation for cunning and contrivance, who had masterminded our gradual recovery from the Depression and who, above all, seemed to possess a unique sensitivity to the peculiar demands of Canadian society? It was. And it was this unlikely paragon who, during the wartime years immediately ahead, never lost sight of the overriding duty of all Canadian prime ministers: to foster national unity. Being a shrewd and observant prime minister, King also knew that, what with a more sophisticated economy and a more demanding populace, national Unity had gone beyond the question of promoting English-French harmony.

But the many virtues of Mr. King (and he was always *Mr.* King) were incidental to my father on whose shoulders I perched. He from Prince Edward Island and my mother from rural Ontario were Liberals born. Politics have always been taken seriously in PEI and rural Ontario. An aunt in Charlottetown would remonstrate with me, during my summer visits there, for playing with children of a neighbouring Conservative family. She pronounced "Conservative" in tones that might more fittingly have been applied to an especially noxious social disease. Of course, some Canadians come to their allegiance through personal taste or the appeal of a specific policy. Others exercise their intellects in an attempt to weigh judiciously the claims of the competing parties. Still others, especially since the advent of television, are heavily influenced by their impression of the leader's personality. Not so my parents. They were genetic Liberals. So, in a sense, was I. Yet these facts alone are hardly enough to justify my offering this little book for public attention.

As I write these words, Canada and the Liberal Party are just now setting forth on a new era following sixteen years of Pierre Trudeau's leadership. In the past, far less dramatic and obvious turning points have provoked a torrent of encomiums, reassessments and recapitulations from political writers of all descriptions, ranging from

9

daily columnists to distinguished scholars. On several occasions the flood has included books written by an observant participant, aimed at the intelligent general reader and dedicated to looking at the party's recent past and probable future (see the bibliography). This is what I am attempting to do here. The Liberals have been in power in Ottawa for all but twenty-one years of the present century. The purpose of this book is to show what Liberal policies have been, especially since the Second World War, and why they resulted in so much public confidence and so many election victories. Doing this leads naturally to a necessary summation of recent events and a prognosis for the future under John Turner's leadership.

That being said, I hope the reader will recognize that, although it is as truthful as I could make it, this book does not claim to be objective. It is, rather, a polemic — full of subjective responses and opinions and arguing a case, trying to win readers over to my viewpoint. Which is perhaps all the more reason why I should begin with some information about myself — beyond the simple facts that I have been proud to represent Etobicoke North in the House of Commons since 1979 and to have sat in cabinet first as Minister of State (Finance) and more recently as Minister of National Revenue. It is perhaps appropriate for me to sketch briefly my own odyssey towards and within the Liberal Party so that the reader can better assess, not only whatever insights I might possess, but my prejudices as well.

While I was growing up, liberalism was simply something in the air, something I caught as one might catch a lifelong and efficacious cold. Yet adolescents are notorious for the short lifespan of their enthusiasms. There were periods, before I was really old enough to understand them very well, when the Liberal sympathies inherited from my parents seemed to fade. After I had put on a few years, I subjected them to searching scrutiny, with probing, silent questions replacing blind acceptance. This makes it sound as though my preference kept fading in and out, like the sound of some distant radio station. In fact, it was less traumatic than that suggests. But I did waver. Then in my late teenage years the original affiliation was reaffirmed when I came to realize that the Liberals had consistently adhered to a simple credo: to protect and to enhance the interests of the many above those of any particular group, and to maximize opportunity for everyone. But I emphasize that all this belief on my part, though genuine enough, was not well articulated or even consciously remembered.

When I went to the University of British Columbia to study history, I did not even join the Liberal Club on campus. While searching in a decidedly prissy and undergraduate way for the eternal verities, I regarded partisan politics, and certainly the activities of such clubs, as slightly vulgar, fleeting and ultimately inconsequential. I was far more interested in what had happened in 1805 than in what was

10

happening in 1955. Yet, at bottom, I continued to believe quietly what I had always believed. And when I went to Cambridge University to do a post-graduate degree, my feelings started coming to the surface. My time there reinforced the conviction, part of the intellectual baggage I carried with me, that liberalism was a good thing. In Canada, it had offered the individual — it had certainly offered me — the opportunity to realize her or his potential. Liberalism was certainly no guarantee that in all cases such potential would be realized, but it offered a greater likelihood of such realization than any other political groove I knew.

Ideas, I found, abound in the Liberal Party, some good, some bad, some brilliant, some absurd. But imagination is never lacking. Hope is the party's hallmark, not fear of change (a chronic malady of Canada's other two major political parties). Eschewing the conventional, the Liberal process of policy formulation is sometimes disorderly, even turbulent, but I soon found that a sort of preliminary accommodation does occur well before legislation is contemplated. Sometimes, as we know from Mackenzie King's diary, this dynamic process irritates party leaders. But its very liveliness makes certain that various points of view are heard and that checks and balances are gradually shaped. I came to understand why, before the Liberal Party assumed its present name, it was called the Reform Party. In other words, I gradually reasoned myself towards my own commitment. The Liberal Party as such was still not the focus of my allegiance. The focus was more blurred, no more than a rather vague if growing attachment to reform through participation. I had become quite certain that John Stuart Mill had been right: "A liberal is he who looks forward for his principles of government; a Tory looks backward." I was certainly pointed in the right direction.

When I graduated from Cambridge, I returned to Canada and joined the Department of External Affairs as a foreign service officer. In the fraternity of External, of course, political involvement was strictly *verboten* and I obeyed the rule religiously. Yet in retrospect I see that my various tours of duty did indeed contribute to my political evolution. In the diplomatic service, including almost five years at the United Nations (and a later spell at Harvard once I'd left External), I became more convinced than ever that the Liberal Party was on the proper course in, for example, promoting Canadian control of Canadian resources. Kipling had asked who knows England who only England knows. I had concluded that, after living in Britain, Vietnam, Czechoslovakia, Switzerland and the United States, I knew something of what Canada was not.

It was not a country where special interests or classes should dominate. If that meant on occasion more government intervention to open greater opportunity, such did not concern me unduly. Indeed, in a bilingual country with a small population and a large territory, collec-

11

tive action appeared the only feasible course. This meant constant negotiation among the two founding races, the provinces and the national government, the regions and the local interests — in short, the practice of compromise. Compromise I had discovered to be a pejorative word in the United States (as befits a republic born in rebellion), but in Canada it seemed to me a good word, given such fresh meaning by King, St. Laurent and Pearson that our country had held together despite formidable centrifugal force. Their empiricism, their willingness to innovate and adapt, which the Liberal Party appeared to embody, appealed to me more and more. Macaulay had been right when he had described liberals as "sanguine in hope, bold in speculation, always pressing forward, quick to discern the imperfection of whatever exists, disposed to think lightly of the risks and inconveniences which attend improvements. . . ." Among such I hoped to number myself.

My reading had made clear that Liberals who, during the early years of this century in both Britain and Canada had sought the enfranchisement of all, rich or poor, male or female, could not be members of a party of particular interests. Such a party naturally attracts a broad membership, thereby helping to ensure its own continuing vitality and regeneration. Once back in Canada, I needed only to look about me to see that millworkers of Quebec, grain farmers of the Prairies, organized labour in Ontario and a wealth of other Canadians have all been active participants. Some have come and some have gone, only to return to the party which has consistently embraced a multiplicity of interests and regarded government as a means of change, of experimentation, of entrepreneurship when there was a reasonable assumption that the private sector alone could or would not achieve the desired end.

So it was — in the 1970s when I had joined the business world in Toronto — that I gradually came to realize that the real power to shape the course of a democratic nation resided largely in political parties and that they, however imperfectly, embody the aspirations of the citizens. Having come to terms with that and made my choices once and for all, it was now important that I become involved in the process.

I took no immediate joy in joining the rather uneven efforts of a local Liberal association in Toronto to better organize itself, to elaborate policies, to attract new members. But gradually I felt better about the whole mundane process. I began to enjoy working with the other members of the Liberal Association of St. Paul's, discussing with them — at least in a desultory way — what we believed could be done to make Canada a better place. At the same time, I began to consider the pleasures and perils of seeking federal office myself (I was never attracted by the municipal or provincial fields). Full of hesitation, I finally decided to take the plunge in 1979.

How I hated ringing doorbells! The uncertainty of the reception. The occasional hostility or the inane challenge. The foetid, over-heated apartments and houses. The barking dogs. The opaque children. But I did at least understand that the only way to win the Liberal nomination in the new constituency of Etobicoke North was to have more supporters at the Liberal nomination meeting than my competitors. St. Paul's, the constituency where I lived, already had nominated a Liberal candidate, but ridings in Metro Toronto did not seem to me very different. My few collaborators and I sought every possible list of past local Liberals, every possible lead to that blessed individual who, for whatever reason, might be willing to give up the major part of a day to elect me the local Liberal candidate in the next federal election. It seemed an awkward and painful means of doing things, this idea of a nomination meeting. But it also seemed better than the alternative, some form of primary in the American manner. But perhaps all candidates feel this way the first time around.

In six weeks the day of the convention finally arrived and thanks largely to the doorbell-ringing, I had there more supporters than any one of my four competitors. Five hours later I heard myself declared the Liberal candidate. Then, in the following weeks and months, a peculiar thing happened. I found that I could ring doorbells without flinching, that I could even enjoy it. On any given day, the first bell would continue to present a fleeting challenge, but once I had begun the doors would open almost magically. A sort of exhilaration at being in a real election race replaced the old shyness, and I chatted quite happily with my would-be constituents.

In an urban constituency, peopled to a substantial degree by recent immigrants, I saw at first hand the gratifying eagerness of New Canadians to participate in building what is still a young and under-developed nation. Frequently, the parents at the door — especially the stay-at-home mothers — spoke little English, but the children were quick to demonstrate their skills, even if they remained vague about what a Member of Parliament is. If no helpful child was at hand, generally the magic name "Trudeau" was sufficient to establish that the mysterious figure at the door must be some sort of politician with a welcome if ill-defined nexus with the revered figure. I discovered that such people work. They find jobs, occasionally even two jobs, and are seldom in my constituency office on a Saturday morning seeking help. Proud and self-reliant, almost all reject any government assistance (which is to say the assistance of other taxpayers). They did not come to Canada to place their names on welfare rolls. They came to work at anything — and most of them do, at least initially.

But there is one constituent — most definitely not a recent immigrant — I remember above all others. She was an elderly woman who happily greeted me at her door. When I announced myself as the local Liberal candidate, she promptly offered to distribute pamphlets or otherwise work on my behalf. She explained that she had first done so for Sir Wilfrid Laurier in the general election of 1911 and was not about to miss the chance in that of 1979. Her face sometimes pops into my memory when I stop to consider the party's earlier years, as one must do if one is to understand the present and to sense the continuity that underlies Liberal politics like a watermark on fine paper.

THE LIBERAL PARTY OF LAURIER AND MACKENZIE KING

Like much else, the ideal of liberalism arrived in Canada in immigrants' baggage. During the early nineteenth century, liberalism in Europe placed prime emphasis on personal freedom and equality of opportunity, which then meant, in its most basic form, equal rights before the law. That is not to say that colonial Canada had been totally "unfree," as the nineteenth century looked at those things, but it was ruled by governors sent from England, assisted by an appointed, not elected, colonial council. These privileged office-holders went by various names. They were the "Family Compact" in Upper Canada (later Ontario) and the "Chateau Clique" in Lower Canada (Quebec). But whatever their name, we can think of them as early conservatives, or Tories, a name they themselves soon adopted. Their liberal opponents,. called Reformers, stood for "responsible government": that is, the principle under which the governor could act only on the advice of ministers who were responsible to a democratically elected house of assembly. In practice this was not the parliamentary democracy which we now enjoy, but it was gradually evolving towards it.

During the 1830s and 1840s, pressure for reform mounted. In this fight for responsible government, the leaders were three remarkable men who can justly be considered the founders of the Liberal Party of Canada: Robert Baldwin, Louis-Hippolyte Lafontaine and George Brown.

Robert Baldwin was in many ways an unlikely Reformer. A Toronto lawyer and a member of the social elite, he was by nature autocratic, reactionary and self-righteous. But he had one obsession for which he was willing to fight with all his strength: responsible government. Louis-Hippolyte Lafontaine, his French-Canadian counterpart, was much more of a political animal, having been elected to the Quebec legislature at age twenty-three. He, too, was an imposing man, with an aloof self-confidence and commanding presence (he looked a little like Napoleon, a resemblance he did nothing to lessen by wearing his hair in the Napoleonic fashion). Yet he was not bellicose. When agitation against the arrogant excesses of the Family Compact and the Chateau Clique boiled over into armed rebellion in 1837, Lafontaine dissociated himself from those advocating violent solutions to French-Canadian grievances. In light of Lord Durham's report on the rebellions, he realized that, if French Canadians were to maintain their rights under British rule, not conflict but co-operation was the better policy. Thus began the momentous alliance between the English-Canadian Baldwin and the French-Canadian Lafontaine under the banner of the Reform Party.

Patiently enduring repeated setbacks, Lafontaine and Baldwin eventually carried Reform to power and in 1849 achieved their goal of responsible government for the united Province of Canada.

But the union of French and English Canadians was an uneasy one. Despite the fact that the population of English Canada was growing with large scale immigration, the province was still only entitled to the same number of legislature seats as Quebec. Accordingly, the cry of "representation by population" arose in Canada West (a cry that had not been heard until English-speaking Canadians clearly began to outnumber French-speaking). "Representation by population" was to be the rallying cry of the third great Reformer, George Brown.

Brown, or "Big Georgie" as his followers called him, was of a different breed altogether; it would have been hard to find more dissimilar men than Brown and Baldwin. A raw-boned, red-headed Scot, Brown had achieved considerable influence through his Liberal newspaper, the Toronto *Globe*. Possessed of enormous energy, he soon made his presence felt after he entered Parliament in 1852. He was a great promoter of westward expansion, seeking to bring the vast lands beyond the Great Lakes into the Canadian union. As a committed Protestant, Brown was passionately dedicated to the separation of church and state, a conviction that brought him into conflict with the French-Canadian Catholics of the Reform Party. Yet for all his fiery speeches and editorials, Brown, like Baldwin before him, came to realize that radicalism and the separation of English and French Canada were not the answers to questions about the future of British North America. When hotheads advocated a dissolution of the union of the two provinces, Brown argued forcefully that Canada should seek to expand, not contract. At the great Reform convention of 1859, he carried all before him, stamping on the Reform movement his leadership and his vision of liberalism in a greater Canada.

Yet there were many battles ahead. Although the Reform Party coalesced behind Brown, the United Canadas remained mired in constitutional deadlock. No government, either Conservative or Reform, could find a way out. By 1863 the best solution increasingly seemed a confederation of all the British North American colonies. The Conservative leaders — George-Etienne Cartier of Quebec and John A. Macdonald of Ontario — were key to the success of the scheme. Even so, the confederation movement would never have got off the ground had it not been for George Brown's commitment.

But it was a changed Brown from the old firebrand. In 1862 he had returned to his native Scotland for an extended holiday. When he returned to Canada, he brought back with him a Scottish bride who had a calming and softening effect on him. He told his supporters that "whenever the great interests of Canada are at risk, we will forget our merely political partisanship and rally round the cause of our coun-

16

try." Brown was as good as his word. His offer in 1864 to his old foe, John Macdonald, to serve in a coalition to achieve confederation was an act of statesmanship and courage. On July 1, 1867, Brown's *Globe,* the bible of Reform, joined church bells and bonfires in hailing the creation of Canada.

In the wake of Confederation, Macdonald's Conservatives basked in glory and formed Canada's first government. Confederation had overnight transformed the political life of British North America; from now on political parties would need to appeal to all Canadians, not just to local interests. Now the task for liberals would be to build a national party. It was to Brown's credit that the Reform group he had cobbled together was to unite into a coherent and forceful party, able to form an effective government in 1873 when Macdonald's was forced to resign over the malodorous Pacific Scandal involving the financing of the Canadian Pacific Railway.

By then a stolid fellow Scot, Alexander Mackenzie, had become the leader of the Reformers, Brown being appointed a senator. A builder by trade, Mackenzie had brought habits of hard work and Calvinist discipline both to Parliament and to the continuation of Brown's work of forging a united Reform party. As Prime Minister, Mackenzie gave the new country sound and reliable government. He introduced the secret ballot at elections, created the Supreme Court and passed the Temperance Act (a measure dear to the hearts of the old Reformers, although not to Sir John A. Macdonald). But Mackenzie's government also had its problems — among them prima donnas in the cabinet, a severe business slump and falling revenues as a result of a global recession. Canadians tended to blame their economic woes on Mackenzie's colourless personality and sought a solution by returning the Conservatives. They remembered Macdonald's gaiety and wit — and forgave him his gin. In 1878 Macdonald swept back into power, and the Liberal Party again had to work out its future from the opposition benches.

Generations of Canadian students have yawned over the question of the tariff. But it was one of *the* issues of Canadian politics all the way from the 1850s to the 1930s; no other issue so clearly distinguished Liberals from Conservatives during the last quarter of the nineteenth century. The Tories, believing that high tariffs were necessary to protect Canada's infant industries, introduced in 1878 their "National Policy" — in a word, protectionism. The next year the tariff wall went up.

The Liberals in opposition crusaded against the policy. Good British Liberal theory told them that free trade was right and protective tariffs wrong. They argued that the Tory tariff smelled of favouritism, putting the interests of manufacturers ahead of the concerns of farmers and consumers. By driving up the price of manufactured goods in Canada, the tariff would distort and slow the natural devel-

17

opment of the economy. The manufacturing industry would indeed grow in the hothouse of the National Policy, but the plan could also kindle social and political conflict, since farmers and consumers would have to pay its costs. The Liberal Party held out the promise of a free trade agreement with the United States as the best course. Such an agreement would create markets hungry for Canada's natural and manufactured products while the bracing winds of competition would keep prices down at home.

Probably the Liberals were naive about the tariff. They did not appreciate that a free trade agreement with the United States could involve a formidable political price. Even if the Americans had been political saints — which they were not — they would have been tempted to ignore or over-ride their weaker partner. Yet Liberals were right to stress that agriculture remained the principal engine of Canadian economic growth. And perhaps no other issue alienated Western Canada more during the next century than the tariff policies the Conservative government had introduced in 1879.

Mackenzie had led the Liberal Party with a stern sense of Calvinistic obligation. Worn and weary when he passed from the scene in 1880, he was replaced by Edward Blake. Highly intelligent and gifted, Blake was never really at home in the rough-and-tumble of the House of Commons. Sometimes his critics felt that he regarded Canada as too small and pedestrian for his many talents. In 1887 Blake resigned as leader and became a Member of Parliament in Britain. The Liberal caucus, following Blake's advice, chose Wilfrid Laurier, the relatively untried member from Quebec, as his successor. This was a gamble, but it proved to be the turning point in the history of the Liberal Party and, indeed, of Canada.

Laurier was forty-six when he became leader. The son of a farming family in St. Lin, Quebec, he had initially opposed Confederation — much of Quebec had — but then came to accept it gradually. A consummate politician, he had mastered the skills of flexibility and compromise essential to Canadian political life; just as important, he loved politics. He throve on the drama of debate. In an age when speeches were a form of entertainment as well as a means of communication, Laurier was a silver-tongued orator. The era of dour Presbyterian leadership in the party had ended. Laurier, with his open, cheerful personality and elegant appearance, was a match for the aging Conservative warrior, Sir John A. Macdonald.

If the tariff was one major contentious issue in Canada in the late nineteenth century, national unity was another. The alienation that French Canadians had always felt under British dominance had not been assuaged by the single act of confederation, even though French Canada's leaders had supported the union. In 1885 an event arose, not in Quebec but in Western Canada, which would sour these relations for decades to come.

18

In the West, dissatisfaction with the National Policy, exacerbated by several years of bad harvests, contributed to increasing resentment. The spark of rebellion was lit by the volatile Métis leader, Louis Riel. With messianic fervour, he led the Métis and Indians against the Canadian government in the North West Rebellion. He was initially successful, but the Indians' small forces were eventually crushed by the Canadian militia, despatched hastily to the West on the new Canadian Pacific Railway. Riel, who had led his men at the Battle of Duck Lake not with a rifle but with a crucifix, was tried for treason and hanged by the neck until dead. His fate and the subsequent dispute in Manitoba over French and Catholic education rights came to symbolize to many in Quebec the English-Canadian threat to the survival of French Canada in Confederation. After 1885 it seemed that two opposing perspectives — one Protestant and English, the other Roman Catholic and French — were on a collision course. French Canada withdrew further into itself.

Laurier's election to the Liberal leadership was, however, a message to Quebec that French and English Canada could in fact live together, and the new leader set out to build the Liberal Party into a potent agent of national unity.

In 1891 Laurier's old opponent — the grand old man of Confederation, Sir John A. Macdonald — died. He had dominated the Conservative Party for so long that it seemed there was no one big enough to step into his shoes. When the Conservatives were starting to pull themselves together with the selection in 1892 of Sir John Thompson as Prime Minister, they suffered another blow. At the early age of fifty, Thompson suddenly died. This time nothing could rally the dispirited Conservative Party. In the election of 1896 the Liberals won a convincing victory. Wilfrid Laurier had become Canada's first French-Canadian Prime Minister.

Laurier was deceptively easy-going, though his urbane, conciliatory exterior hid great strength. He now set about consolidating the Liberals in power and building up party support all across the country. Never again should the party have to be in the wilderness of opposition while the Conservatives posed as the party of Confederation, patriotism and the people (and, one might add, of patronage). So Laurier constructed his cabinet carefully. It was to be the strongest and most regionally balanced cabinet to date, a model for all future cabinet-makers. It included five former premiers while from Manitoba came the young Clifford Sifton.

With a French-Canadian Prime Minister in office, francophone resentment gradually died down, at least for the time being. But soon another threat to national unity arose. Most English Canadians took pride in the British Empire, and when Britain went to war in South Africa in 1899 they clamoured to participate. French Canadians were indifferent, if not downright opposed, seeing the Boers (some of whom were of French ancestry) as fighting for their freedom against foreign conquest. Laurier's cabinet was badly divided. The Prime Minister eventually evolved an uneasy compromise whereby volunteers were enabled to go but once in South Africa were to be paid by Britain. Protests from French Canada faded when Laurier won re-election in 1900, but the issue of Canada's imperial connection would not go away. It was to be revived when the question of Canada's contribution to her own incipient naval defences came up in 1910 and would even further fracture Canada's shaky unity during the First World War.

At home Sir Wilfrid Laurier was busy nation-building. Like George Brown before him, he understood the importance of opening up the West — to fill the empty spaces towards which some American politicians were casting hungry glances. Clifford Sifton, Laurier's Minister of the Interior and himself a westerner, was an enthusiastic booster of the glorious pioneering opportunities available across the prairies. Under his energetic leadership, pamphlets and advertisements in many languages formed part of an enormous promotional campaign, and paid agents ranged through Europe. Such efforts were unbelievably successful. During the Laurier years, as the United States frontier came to an end, over two million European and American immigrants flocked to Western Canada. Two transcontinental railways were pushed across the nation whether needed or not. And in 1905 Laurier created the new provinces of Alberta and Saskatchewan.

But the boom in the West posed new problems. Prairie farmers complained about the high costs of transporting their crops to distant markets. In 1897, Laurier responded with the Crow's West Pass agreement which guaranteed low freight rates for their grain. Nevertheless, westerners believed that the high tariffs benefitted Ontario and Quebec at their expense. In part to meet their demands, Laurier in 1911 made a favourable "reciprocity" agreement with the United States, involving tariff concessions between the two countries. Eastern manufacturers responded by throwing their support to the Conservatives. The Tories, seeing in trade reciprocity a sell-out to the United States, threatened to blockade Parliament. In 1911 Laurier called an election. Laurier was defeated by an unholy combination of English-Canadian imperialists and French-Canadian ultra-nationalists, supported by a coalition of provincial premiers with grievances against the federal government.

During its subsequent years in opposition, from 1911 to 1921, the Liberal Party was battered. In particular, the First World War increased the strains on the nation. The Conservatives were able to draw on a surge of imperialist sentiment in English Canada as young men rushed to fight for the British Empire in the "war to end all wars." Under the aggressive if confused Sam Hughes, the brash Minister of Militia and Defence, Canadian troops found themselves transported to Europe to endure, or to die, in the mud of Flanders. The British generals' only response to the stalemate of trench warfare seemed to be to pour in even more men. Faced with insatiable demands for more soldiers, in 1917 the Conservative Prime Minister, Sir Robert Borden, introduced conscription for overseas service. Laurier, who had consistently supported the war effort in every other way, knew that conscription would sorely test national unity and might even spark violent conflict between English and French Canada. He opposed it. But not even Laurier, the master of compromise, could maintain the shaky balance within the Liberal Party. Quebec Liberals dug in their heels against conscription while many prominent Liberals in English Canada, having broken with Laurier's position, were wooed into Borden's Union Government. In the general election which followed, the Tories hoped to wipe the Liberals off the map. They almost succeeded but, although bruised and shaken, the Liberal Party held on. Most of its MPs were from Quebec, but not all. It was still, precariously, a national party. With Laurier's death in 1919, Liberals looked to a national convention for impetus to carry on his work.

The Liberal Party had to do more than heal its wounds. The Great War of 1914-18 had shaken some of the comfortable assumptions about Canadian life. Canada had become an industrial nation, but the government had yet done little to alleviate abuses of an industrial society. As the nation passed uneasily from war to peace, some wondered if the social fabric would hold. In Western Canada, farmers increased their demands for reform. Labour and capital seemed headed for crippling confrontation. Radical protest parties flourished. Just before the Liberal convention, Winnipeg was gripped by a general strike. So in 1919 the Liberal Party had to repair itself, rally around a new leader and offer new approaches to achieve national and social harmony.

The 1919 convention endorsed the basic Liberal platform on trade, as it had been since 1897, and put the party squarely on the side of progressive reform, including a programme of social welfare. The candidate chosen as Laurier's successor was William Lyon Mackenzie King, grandson of the fiery leader of the 1837 rebellion in Upper Canada.

The image many Canadians now have of King is that of the lonely bachelor who adored his mother, doted on his dog and communicated with the spirit world. These are facts, but they tell us little that is useful about how King led Canada for almost thirty years. In fact, he was one of the best and brightest of his generation. As a student in Canada and the United States in the 1890s, King threw himself into the study of industrial conditions and labour relations. He brought his considerable talents and knowledge to Ottawa in 1900, soon becoming the first deputy minister of Labour and winning renown as a concilia-

21

tor. Having entered Parliament in 1908, King was made Minister of Labour the following year. Defeated in 1911, he returned to private life, serving for a time as John D. Rockefeller's advisor on industrial relations. He ran successfully as a Laurier Liberal (against conscription) in 1917.

Some decry King as a dull, bumbling, indecisive fuddy-duddy. He was frequently, though not invariably, a dull speaker. Yet as a relatively young leader, he kept order in his party, pacifying the aging ones who believed that *they* should be leaders and keeping the young at bay, if not at rest. This was no mean accomplishment.

In rebuilding the party, King's first task was to repair the painful fractures of the conscription crisis. With great tact, he moved at just the right pace to draw conscriptionist Liberals back into the party. At the same time, the suspicious anti-conscriptionists, who had stood loyally with Laurier, were coaxed out of their shells. The uneasy tension between the two groups gradually dissolved in the face of the common challenge of party construction. King healed the wounds not a moment too soon: in 1921, the Conservatives collapsed under their own dead weight and the Liberal Party, repaired and revitalized, won the election.

Now Prime Minister, King had to face a new challenge to national unity. Farmer protest, aroused by the Conservative tariff, had found a powerful voice in the new Progressive Party, which won sixty-five seats in the 1921 election, fifteen more than the outgoing Conservatives. In the ferment immediately after the war, the Progressives toppled provincial governments in Alberta and Ontario and between 1921 and 1926 held the balance of power in Ottawa as well. King believed that the Liberal Party was the vehicle for reconciling the competing claims of the various groups and regions. In cabinet, in caucus and in the party as a whole, he would solicit opinion, find common ground and almost invariably strike the right balance of policies. He had learned this essential lesson of Liberal statecraft from Laurier but he was drawing also upon his own experience as a labour mediator.

King believed that the Progressives were really Liberals at heart: the two parties shared a common tradition of free trade and opposition to high tariffs. During the 1920s, King kept the channels of communication with the Progressives open, inviting their leaders to ally themselves with Liberal policies. There was no magic reconciliation, but King's skilful management of the Progressive challenge helped to preserve the delicate balance of national unity.

The 1920s brought a surge of prosperity. To create a climate of confidence and help pay off the staggering war debt, King promised lean, efficient administration. Governments in the 1920s, of whatever political colour, had only a small role in managing the economy and tried to diminish even that. Large budgets were associated only with wartime, deficits were sinful — a sign of financial irresponsibility. At budget time, Finance ministers were expected to keep the account books neat, tidy and in the black. The less government did, apart from paying the national debt, the better. The Liberal Party shared this restricted view of fiscal management. As a result, those who expected the 1919 Liberal platform of welfare and social security to be enacted overnight were disappointed. King's commitment to social reform and social security was profound, but he viewed the promises of 1919 as long-term goals to be implemented over time, as opportunities when the federal budget permitted.

There were also constitutional obstacles standing in the way of Liberal social reform. Under the BNA Act, the provinces were responsible for welfare and social services. If Ottawa were to act, the consent of the provinces and a lengthy process of constitutional amendment would be necessary. There had been enough squabbling between the federal government and the provinces since Confederation. King did not want to arouse again the prickly sensibilities of "provincial rights." Constitutional calm could best be maintained if the two levels of government remained in their own backyards. King did venture, however, to win provincial support for the national Old Age Pensions Act in 1927. It was a major achievement, the first step on the long road to a system of national social security.

Some Conservatives had never lost hope that the British Empire could be altered to give Canada and her sister dominions formal participation in an imperial foreign policy. But King and other Liberals, schooled in the tradition of Laurier, were sceptical. The vision of an imperial federation was for them a pipe dream. King correctly saw Britain as an imperial power with global interests which were not necessarily Canada's. Imperial entanglements, as Liberals knew too well, could call up a parade of ghosts from Canada's past and set English and French Canadians at one another. And so under King's leadership, Canada moved slowly towards the full autonomy which Laurier had foreseen and his Conservative successor, Sir Robert Borden, had initiated during the war.

An important if mundane step in that direction came in 1923 with the Halibut Fisheries Treaty with the United States. No one seemed to notice that Canada signed the innocuous-sounding treaty without a concurrent British signature, but King pressed home the symbolic significance. Canada had now assumed fully the right to negotiate, sign and ratify her own treaties without the participation of Britain.

In 1926, at an imperial conference, the new spirit of dominion status was again confirmed. In fact, King feared that the conference was moving a little too quickly: he wanted the Empire to evolve gradually so that its collective identity would be strengthened, not eroded, by the new equal status of the dominions. Governing in the shadow of decades of national debate, he was determined to nudge

23

Canada towards a view of her place in the world which would not threaten national unity at home. On a more positive note, he dispatched Canadian legations to Washington, Paris and Tokyo. Soon King and his trusted advisor, O.D. Skelton, the under-secretary of state for External Affairs, recruited the first of an outstanding generation of Canadian diplomats (among whom was a young history professor from Toronto, Lester Pearson).

Governments in power during hard times seldom fare well at the polls. In 1930 the Depression hit home. Despite its considerable accomplishments during the heady 1920s, the Liberal government was defeated. Naturally King did not want to lose, but the fact that the Liberal Party was out of office for the next five years proved to be a godsend. King and his colleagues watched from the sidelines as R.B. Bennett's Conservatives bumbled their way through the first years of the Depression. To be fair, governments in the early 1930s, faced with unparalleled economic difficulties, did not know which way to turn and simply muddled along as best they could. In 1930, even King had offered no better solution than some assistance to the provinces for welfare and a tightening of the federal money belt.

In opposition, King prepared for the day when Canada would reject Bennett at the polls. In 1933, the party convened a "summer conference" (not a convention) and offered some timely ideas on the problems of the day, including a reaffirmation of the commitment to lower tariffs, efficient and cost-conscious administration, and a national commission to untangle the confusion of employment relief. In 1932 the Co-operative Commonwealth Federation (CCF), the precursor of today's NDP, had been formed in Regina by a coalition of radical farmer movements, socialist groups and intellectuals. There was little temptation for Liberals to raid the policies of the CCF since the Liberal Party had long before put itself on the side of welfare and social security. The CCF was less a threat and more a reminder that Liberals had to offer a better assurance of the future than either Conservatives or socialists could provide.

By 1935, economic conditions had not much improved. Bennett, in a last effort to shore up the slumping credibility of his government and without consulting either his cabinet or party, introduced his own version of Franklin Roosevelt's New Deal. King shared the spirit behind Bennett's intent, but rightly warned that many of the Tory schemes would end in constitutional hot water. In any event, Bennett's death-bed conversion to such "radical" policies failed to convince Canadians. The Prime Minister forfeited what little authority he still had in the nation. He forfeited even the respect of some of his own ministers who told King, not him, of their troubles. Many Canadians, frustrated and angry, turned to protest parties offering magical cures. In the summer of 1935, some of the unemployed began an "on-to-Ottawa trek." It was met with force initially and later petered out, but many Canadians remained profoundly concerned that things were getting out of hand. And so in the election of 1935 the Liberal Party offered "King or chaos." Canadians chose King.

After putting together a solid, nationally balanced cabinet, King turned to the Depression crisis. Bennett's relief camps were abolished, replaced partly by subsidies to the railways to hire unemployed on repair and construction projects. King met with the provincial premiers and offered more federal help to meet the mounting costs of relief. Concurrently, an important trade agreement with the United States did something to reduce skyrocketing tariffs (three years later, it was followed with a broader three-way agreement involving Britain as well as the United States). In 1936, King established the National Employment Commission to supervise unemployment relief and to propose new approaches. The Bank of Canada Act was introduced to make it publicly controlled. The promises of 1933 and 1935 had been met. But still the Depression did not go away.

King hoped that even in the Depression federal spending could be kept under tight control and that the provinces alone would be able to meet most if not all the costs of relief. By 1935, these hopes had clearly become illusory. Before long, Manitoba and Saskatchewan were on the edge of bankruptcy. Alberta was in default on its public debt. There was now no choice but for Ottawa to bail them out. Slowly, too slowly, the federal government moved towards a more expanded view of its responsibilities. There were still many old Liberals in the cabinet, including King himself, who wanted to hold down federal spending. But there were also more vocal advocates of greater spending to stimulate the economy. True to form, King struck a compromise between these two groups in his cabinet. In the 1938 budget, the restraints on spending were cautiously removed. No one then understood the importance of this breakthrough (Keynes was not yet acknowledged as the master) but Liberals were feeling their way towards a bolder concept of the government's role in the management of the economy.

There were still many obstacles in the way of national leadership. In Alberta, Premier William (Bible Bill) Aberhart sold the magical nostrums of Social Credit over the radio and passed laws which not only infringed on federal responsibility for banking but also defied common sense. Aberhart's strange spiritual-monetary pilgrimage would have wrecked Alberta's fiscal stability and undermined the confidence of the national financial community if King had not disallowed the Social Credit legislation. When it reappeared, King referred it to the Supreme Court which ruled against the acts. King played tough with Aberhart, and Aberhart backed down.

In Quebec, Maurice Duplessis had risen to power in 1936 on a potent mixture of progressive ideas and strident French-Canadian nationalism. He soon jettisoned the progressive ideas and settled in as an exponent of conservative nationalism. Duplessis joined with Mitchell Hepburn, Ontario's Liberal premier, in a war of confrontation with Ottawa. Their intense hostility made it all the more difficult to handle the national economic crisis. In 1937, for example, King reluctantly sought provincial agreement for federal unemployment insurance. The provinces were suspicious, leaving King no choice but to sit tight. Only in the very different wartime circumstances of 1940 would the provinces finally consent. There were signs enough in the late 1930s that the financial arrangements arising from the BNA Act were in need of drastic revision. But as long as Aberhart, Duplessis and Hepburn saw federal-provincial relations as a form of trench warfare, there was little that King could do. In 1937, however, he established the Rowell-Sirois Royal Commission on federal-provincial relations (whose legal counsel included an eminent Quebec lawyer, Louis St. Laurent) to recommend fiscal arrangements that would better accord with the demands of an increasingly industrial state, especially one experiencing the turmoil of a depression.

As the Dirty Thirties ended, the Depression still weighed heavily on the nation. There were, however, strong signs of new national leadership and determination in Ottawa, though King had not won the affection of the Canadian people: his style of leadership was too mundane for that — but he was in firm command of his government.

In the field of international affairs, after 1935, Mackenzie King's main concern was Canada's role in the League of Nations. Canada had been a founding member in 1919 but during the 1920s, King, like most Canadians, was wary of the League. He conceded that an organization which encouraged nations to talk out their problems was all to the good. But the League advocated "collective security" — a common defence against aggression — and that smelled of involvement in events in which Canada had little or no influence. Besides, the United States had not joined the League. The Liberal Party shared the isolationist mood of the nation. Then in 1935 the Italian dictator Mussolini attacked Ethiopia. Before Mackenzie King resumed the post of Prime Minister, Canada had joined in the call for sanctions against Italy. King was willing to support sanctions, but urged the Canadian delegate in Geneva to keep his head down and repudiated him when he did not.

The Ethiopian crisis had dealt a death blow to the League of Nations. It had not been one of King's finer moments, but perhaps it would have been naive to expect Canada to play a larger role. Certainly King knew that Canada's foreign policy could go no further than the national will behind it. It is only in hindsight, too, that we can see how the paralysis of the League and the diplomacy of appeasement led to war. Even with his occult insights, King was no better than most of his contemporaries at predicting the future. Nevertheless, despite considerable opposition in his cabinet and in the nation, he boosted Canada's modest defence spending in 1936 and 1938.

By 1939, war was rapidly approaching, although many shared King's view that this crisis too would somehow be surmounted. Pearson, on leave during the summer of 1939 from his post in London, thought otherwise. He would later write: "I told Mr. King that I was convinced war was near and therefore I planned to return to London immediately. He thought that I was wrong, that this crisis too would be resolved. He had seen Hitler not so long before and did not think he would risk a general war . . . . He was one among millions who felt that way. Another world war was unthinkable!" Yet it was King who led Canada triumphantly through that unthinkable world war.

On September 10, 1939, Canada went to war for the second time in less than thirty years. Overnight the job of governing changed dramatically. During the next six years Canada itself was transformed. For many Canadians, especially the young men who poured into the recruiting offices, the war meant uniforms, food, a bed every night and free medical care. When war was declared, there were fewer than ten thousand men in uniform; five years later more than one million men and women would be in the forces. For them and for those who found employment in new factories, in the mines and forests and on farms, the despair of the Depression began to fade.

The war effort would require unprecedented federal spending. That meant abandoning, for the moment, distinctions between federal and provincial taxing powers. When the Rowell-Sirois Commission finally reported in 1940 with sweeping proposals to strike a new fiscal balance between levels of government, some provinces were still in desperate financial shape. The war made the need for change all the more urgent. In the emergency, the federal government took over the taxing powers of the provinces until the end of the war.

To fight the war, the rules and rhythms of a normal peacetime economy had to be set aside. With the sudden fall of France in 1940, Canadian industry rapidly geared up to produce shells, guns, aircraft, ships and a myriad of other equipment, much of it novel to the Canadian manufacturing industry. To ensure the greatest war contribution (Canada was the second strongest power fighting Hitler during the perilous months from mid-1940 until mid-1941), Mackenzie King's government introduced rationing as well as controls on prices, wages and foreign exchange. Mindful of the inflation and profiteering of the First World War, King and his colleagues sought to ensure equitable rules for the new war effort.

As the order books of industry lengthened, the flow of production had to be supervised and controlled. King was fortunate to have just the man for the job. C.D. Howe was a New Englander who had come to Canada in 1908 to teach engineering and had later moved to the Lakehead to set up his own construction business. When he won

27

the riding of Port Arthur for the Liberals in 1935, King immediately put him into the cabinet; Howe had no parliamentary experience, but King recognized that his driving force, his organizational skills and his good relations with the business community were valuable assets. It was these same assets that he called upon now to mastermind the war effort. As Minister of Munitions and Supply, Howe quickly appointed comptrollers to monitor the flow of scarce resources to industry. Crown corporations were created to do whatever private business could not. Mostly by example — though occasionally by fiat — Howe got the best from both those who worked for him and from the business community generally. Industrial production increased dramatically.

But Canada's contribution to the Allied cause could not rest on war production alone, however much King hoped it might. Hundreds of thousands of Canadians volunteered for active service in the army, air force and navy and fought bravely and effectively in Europe and Asia. Eventually, however, the dreaded, divisive issue of conscription again surfaced. King now applied a lifetime of political experience to ensure that national unity would not once more be imperilled. Early in the war, all political parties opposed conscription for overseas service. Such service would be filled entirely by volunteers. Under the National Resources Mobilization Act of 1940, eligible Canadians could be conscripted for home defence only. By 1942, however, it had become clear that the war would be long, costly and, after the Japanese attack on Pearl Harbor, global as well. The possibility of conscription for overseas service could not be ignored, and the Conservative Party reversed its previous position. There was no easy way out of the dilemma now facing King. On the one hand, if the government also reversed its promise and embraced conscription, national unity would be put directly at risk. If, on the other hand, the necessary reinforcements for units overseas were unavailable once numerous casualties were incurred, Canada's contribution to the Allied war effort could be impaired. Always a master of compromise and timing, King steered between these two poles. To avoid confrontation, he called in 1942 for a national plebiscite to release the government "from any obligation arising out of any past commitment restricting the methods of raising men for military service." But characteristically no specific commitment to conscription was made. It would be "not necessarily conscription, but conscription if necessary," as King with great deliberation put it. The Prime Minister and his colleagues campaigned diligently to win support for this moderate option. In Quebec, the Liberal Party, including King's new lieutenant, Louis St. Laurent, tried to soothe anti-conscriptionist suspicions. The result of the plebiscite was unsatisfactory but hardly surprising. English Canada overwhelmingly supported the government's request but French Canada equally decisively rejected it. The National Resources Mobilization Act was amended, following a two-month debate, to allow home defence troops to be sent overseas. With volunteering countinuing at high levels, there was no need to do so. King prayed that it would never become necessary.

By late 1944, however, mounting Canadian losses in Europe raised the prospect of inadequate reinforcements. King faced a split in his cabinet: the Minister of National Defence, Colonel Ralston, on visiting the troops in Europe, found confirmation of a potential reinforcement crisis. Returning to Canada, Ralston, an able and conscientious man, pressed for overseas conscription and won the support of some of his colleagues. Several other of King's ministers, however, remained sceptical, if not adamantly opposed. No matter which way King turned, it seemed that he would be faced with ministerial resignations and probably with those of the chiefs of the General Staff as well. He resuscitated a forgotten letter of resignation from Ralston, quickly appointing the widely respected General Andrew McNaughton in Ralston's place. No cabinet resignations ensued, and King eventually allowed a few conscripts to be sent overseas. And as it turned out, with the end of fighting in Europe rapidly approaching, not as many home service troops had to be sent overseas as had been predicted.

As the Allied victory hove into view, there was much popular interest in reconstruction and security for the postwar world. No one wanted a repetition of the uncertainty which Canadians had experienced at the end of the First World War; no one wanted Canada to relive the bleak days of the Depression. Even before the production of shells and aircraft started to wind down, the printing presses were humming with books, pamphlets and editorials about the "quest for security" in the postwar world. The Liberal government had to find answers, and quickly, as lost by-elections and adverse opinion polls proved.

Having spent the last months of 1943 defining its postwar agenda, the government outlined, in the Speech from the Throne in early 1944, a far-ranging approach to reconstruction. Three new departments — National Health and Welfare, Veterans Affairs, and Reconstruction — were created. King introduced a sweeping Veterans' Charter to assist returning soldiers to find employment and security. A National Housing Act offered low-interest mortgages to bring home ownership within reach of the average Canadian. But the most dramatic advance in the quest for security came with the Family Allowance Act. It provided a so-called baby bonus to all mothers, thus boosting the earnings of low-income families, and soon became a symbol of the Liberal commitment to welfare. Although the Conservatives at least knew better than to oppose family allowances when the bill came to a final vote in the House, many prominent Tories spoke against it, calling it, among other things, a political bribe to the large (and anti-conscriptionist) families of Quebec. The Liberal Party moved ahead with its plan for increased social security. The Tories fell behind.

In 1945, national attention turned to an even more urgent question: what would happen to Canada's economy during the transition to peace? Many feared that the dynamic wartime economy would falter. Howe shared no such doubts. It was wrong, he was convinced, to assume that the national government would have to intervene massively. The reconstruction of the economy, had, in fact, begun during the war, when industry had been overhauled and greatly expanded. A new generation of managers and a workforce of unprecedented skill would provide the expertise to retool for peace time. Canadians had enjoyed full employment and good wages during the war; inflation had been kept low. With lots to spend, consumer demand would spur additional industrial conversion and expansion. Even before hostilities had ended, Ottawa offered tax incentives to speed the change to peacetime production. Quietly and skilfully, Howe supervised the dismantling of wartime controls, including the sale of many crown corporations.

Howe's predictions for unprecedented economic prosperity would turn out to be right. But not all Canadians fully shared his optimism, and the Liberals would soon have to face an election. Canadians wanted to know what their government would do if the worst should occur and the economy suffer a relapse. To answer that question, Howe's staff prepared a white paper on employment and income. It assured Canadians that their government would guide and, if necessary, intervene in the economy to maintain "a high and stable level of employment," a term the press soon shortened to "full employment." The paper also stressed the role of private investment, science and technology and — if necessary — planning. By 1945 more people were putting more faith into national planning than ever before.

The Liberal platform for the 1945 election was a sober compromise between the free pre-war attitude and proposals to nationalize everything in sight espoused by the socialist idealists of the CCF. This compromise platform was sufficiently appealing to the electorate to give King and his colleagues a narrow majority in the House of Commons (to his chagrin, King was defeated in his own riding but was soon elected in another).

The new administration turned first to the perennially vexing issue of federal-provincial relations. With the war ending, the wartime tax arrangements would also end. Until the fundamental matter of taxation was cleared up, little could be done on other economic and social fronts. King called a federal-provincial conference for 1945, with St. Laurent supervising preparation of the federal position. The conference convened on August 6, 1945. That morning, King received word that an atom bomb had been dropped on Hiroshima and so informed the startled premiers. Now with the end of the Pacific war only days away, the business of the conference became all the more urgent. King and St. Laurent outlined the broad national perspective in a surprisingly short and clear pamphlet, bound in green, which became famous (at least among civil servants and academics) as the Green Book.

There could be no return to anything resembling the *laissez-faire* of the Depression years. The Green Book represented something of a revolution in Liberal policy, with state intervention considered necessary to enhance the liberty of the individual, including help to ensure the well being of society's weaker members. The absence of food, shelter, or medical care was just as much a threat to individual liberty as any government restrictions. Accordingly, the party committed itself to achieving a welfare state in which redistribution of income would be compatible with the liberty of the individual. Collective action would maximize individual opportunity.

The 1945 Green Book proposed increasing federal spending on pensions, health and unemployment insurance, job training and rehabilitation, and public works. There would be further spending for provincial services and the development of natural resources. All in all, it was a large agenda. To carry it out, King asked the provinces to "rent" Ottawa the field of personal and corporate income taxes and succession duties in exchange for annual payments. The pot was made sweet: the provinces would enjoy a fifty per cent increase in revenue over the existing wartime arrangements. The Green Book offered a strong national vision. But some provincial premiers, it seemed, were colour blind. George Drew, the Tory premier of Ontario, and Duplessis, the ex-Tory premier of Quebec, combined to scuttle the conference. Ottawa sweetened the pot even further, but subsequent talks in 1946 again failed. The next year King offered a modified and voluntary tax proposal to the provinces. It would avoid overlapping taxes and centralize tax collection. Seven provinces soon joined in, but Ontario and Quebec went their separate ways.

For the moment at least the Liberal Party had put aside the ambitious programme of the Green Book. It remains, however, a surprising document. Unlike most government documents, it is remarkably readable. More importantly, it contains in its few pages much of the agenda of Liberal government during the three decades from 1945 to 1975. That was the good news. The bad was that the federal-provincial conference of 1945 became a public circus of intergovernmental discord. King would not convene another, but federal-provincial discord would remain a major item on the agenda.

Mackenzie King's retirement in 1948 brought to an end an extraordinarily successful career of public service. Many wondered then, as they still do, how that pudgy, lonely man with a penchant for spiritualism had governed so skilfully for so long. The answer, perhaps, can be found in King's unwavering sense of what was necessary to ensure the integrity of the nation. His commitment to national unity and consensus knew no bounds. Patient, cautious but ever persistent, he never faltered in his conviction that the values of liberalism — tolerance, compromise, opportunity and freedom — were the foundations of Canada's unity and strength. For King, the Liberal Party was the agent of unity and Liberals would always be found at the cutting edge of progress and reform. Just as important was his keen eye for competency in government. An extraordinary generation of gifted cabinet ministers and public servants had matched the great achievement of the war effort with the success of the postwar quest for security. Now, as a decade of war and reconstruction under King's leadership drew to a close, St. Laurent, Howe, Pearson and their colleagues were ready to govern with the same conviction and energy. King's final contribution to Canada and his party was the careful thought that he had given to his own succession.

THE LIBERAL PARTY AND THE POSTWAR WORLD ECONOMY

As the Second World War drew to a close, the Liberal government looked to the creation of a new, stable world economic order to help lead the country into postwar prosperity. No one could forget the stultifying grip of the Depression. The best way to achieve economic growth at home was to make certain the world did not slip back into the futile tariff disputes of the pre-war years.

The war had done much to change Canadian attitudes. The country had played a vital part in the Allied war effort; her armed forces had served with distinction in the liberation of Europe. Gone finally was the old spirit of isolationism. The Liberals, in common with the majority of Canadians, realized that the road to postwar security lay in international co-operation and the establishment of sturdy international institutions to prevent the disastrous failure of previous politicians to avoid world conflagration. As Louis St. Laurent was to say in 1947, "If there is one conclusion that our common experience has led us to accept, it is that security for this country lies in the development of a firm structure of international organization."

By the end of the war, Canada's external policies were passing to younger hands. In 1946 an increasingly weary Mackenzie King handed over the External Affairs portfolio to St. Laurent. When King resigned as Prime Minister, St. Laurent replaced him and Lester Pearson became Secretary of State for External Affairs. The transition from the old diplomacy of King and his advisor O.D. Skelton to the new international diplomacy of St. Laurent and Pearson had begun.

St. Laurent was King's choice as his successor. A French Canadian, he was popular with both French and English Canadians and understood the problems of national unity to a unique degree. Courtly and warm-hearted, St. Laurent sometimes gave the impression of an amateur in politics, a successful lawyer who had entered public life only late in life. In fact, he was a remarkably shrewd statesman. The nickname Uncle Louie came to reflect the affection and esteem in which Canadians held him.

Pearson's path to a political career had been markedly different; he was to be one of the first of a series of brilliant civil servants the Liberal Party was able to attract to government. Mike, as he was called, had started his career as a history professor at the University of Toronto and in 1928 joined the Department of External Affairs, spending much of the war in London. Pearson's obvious talents as a conciliator and his experience in foreign affairs made him the natural choice to succeed St. Laurent at External Affairs. Possessed of great charm, he was an immediate asset to the new Prime Minister, skilfully using his mastery of the intricacies of foreign policy to guide Canada into a more active role in the new world order.

Even during the war, Canada had learned how to hold her own on the world stage. By virtue of the importance of her contribution to the war effort, Canada had a vital stake in most Allied planning committees and, on a few, played a major role. But Canadians were realistic enough to know that they could not expect status equal to that of the so-called great powers. There was, however, one simple strategy which offered a way by which Canada could win influence or play a part as a "middle power." In the North Atlantic triangle, Canada was placed between Britain and the United States. Tied by history to both, Canada could attempt to interpret one to the other, hoping thereby to help draw them together. There was more than a touch of idealistic conceit in this self-appointed role, but since what Britain and the United States did was crucial to Canada's own national interests, the attempt was hardly surprising. During the war, the Liberal government had deployed its new participatory diplomacy with success. Now it could be applied to give Canada some leverage in the wider search for international security and prosperity.

Before the war had ended, Canada and her allies had looked ahead to the creation of a new and better world organization to replace the discredited League of Nations. It was natural that the great powers should take the prime responsibility for planning the United Nations. Canada was largely on the sidelines, but the Liberal government generally cheered on the progress of the negotiations and, whenever possible, intervened to ensure that the new body would not become just another club for global powers. An all-party delegation attended the San Francisco conference where the UN Charter was forged in 1945. By this time, the government had acknowledged, at least to itself, that the UN would not be a *perfect* international organization. In fact, King feared that the great powers had too much influence and that the UN would entangle Canada in commitments over which it had too little control. St. Laurent shared the more realistic view advanced by Pearson and the Department of External Affairs that without the commitment of the great powers, the credibility of the UN would suffer. At San Francisco, the Canadian delegation was especially concerned that the UN's role in collective security did not seem well enough defined. Accordingly, the delegation strove to make the machinery as workable and flexible as possible; once the UN was launched, perhaps the leaks could be plugged and the ballast shifted. What sort of clout the UN would have, and to what degree middle powers like Canada would be able to influence its further evolution, remained questions for the future.

A second objective of Canada's postwar foreign policy was to foster European security. After the German surrender in 1945, an increasingly hostile Soviet Union consolidated its control of eastern

Europe, posing a new threat to peace and stability, especially since the Western allies had largely disarmed themselves. As the Iron Curtain descended across the continent, relations chilled between the Soviet Union and the West. Canadians had already been made aware of these new harsh realities when, in 1945, a cypher clerk in the Soviet Embassy in Ottawa exposed an espionage ring operating in Canada, Britain and the United States. In 1948, a communist *coup d'état* in Czechoslovakia and a Soviet blockade of the Allied zones of Berlin, deep in the Russian sector of Germany, drove home the necessity for a more concerted response.

True to form, the cautious Mackenzie King did not like the idea of involving Canada in a defence alliance with Europe and the United States. But St. Laurent and Pearson chose the route of greater international commitment. They put Canada's full weight behind the creation of the North Atlantic Treaty Organization. The United Nations unfortunately was proving too weak to play any substantial role in the crucial question of European security. Regional arrangements, as provided for in the UN Charter, would have to be relied on for the foreseeable future. As NATO took shape, Pearson hoped that it would be more than a simple military alliance. He pressed for a broader economic and cultural agreement among its members. Perhaps he was being idealistic. In his mind, the Atlantic alliance was built on the values of justice and democracy, the common heritage of European civilization. But he was being more hard-headed than he at first seemed, as economic and cultural ties would strengthen the identity of NATO and sharpen its members' collective resolve. Canada's proposals were included as article two of the treaty and then, to Pearson's subsequent distress, soon forgotten.

But even the brightest and best of international organizations (and not even its most ardent fans would claim the United Nations was that) would be powerless in the face of economic chaos and rampant protectionism. The nations of the West would also have to learn to work together in terms of international trade. If the momentum of wartime co-operation and planning was lost, channels of trade would silt up and many countries, Canada among them, could suffer a crippling financial crisis.

The first step in the calling into being of a new economic order was the creation of the International Monetary Fund at Bretton Woods in 1944. In light of her wartime effort, Canada enjoyed a privileged role during the negotiations, with her representatives working to smooth the way to an accord between Britain and the United States. The IMF became a permanent institution, originally intended to promote orderly exchange rates among national currencies, a necessary pre-condition for growth in international trade.

But though the IMF pointed the way to a stabilization of world trade, the road to international security remained tortuous. During the war, massive expenditures by their governments distorted the financial relations of Canada, Britain and the United States. Britain had simply run out of US dollars to pay for purchases of necessary war supplies. Canada and the United States had provided Britain with assistance under the wartime lend-lease agreements but at the end of the war Britain was on the brink of bankruptcy. More than sentiment stirred the Liberal government to act; if Britain's already precarious situation worsened, Canada would be hurt, too, postponing the international adjustment to peacetime. Towards the end of the war, Ottawa had juggled British indebtedness to Canada and then offered a generous loan to ease Britain's immediate financial crisis. In 1946, the loan helped bring some stability to Britain.

The new International Monetary Fund provided one pillar in the search for postwar security. Now what was needed was a similar international agreement to get trade moving again and to avoid the vicious tariff conflicts of the 1930s. In 1947, Canada joined in the negotiation, in Havana, of the General Agreement on Tariffs and Trade (GATT), knowing that it had everything to gain from the reduction or elimination of trade barriers to which all signatories pledged themselves.

The fostering of Canadian-American trade was much on the minds of the Liberal government when the IMF and GATT were established. As Canadians knew all too well, Americans have been prone to frequent protectionist spasms. Much of Canada's trade policy, back to the middle of the nineteenth century, has been in reaction to protectionist thinking in the United States. Canada thus had much to gain by encouraging the Americans to bind themselves to the IMF and GATT, and thus to the defence of a new international trading order. Greater access to world markets and more stable access to the US market in particular were the twin goals of the Liberal government; in their view such a strategy was the only guarantee of prosperity.

In 1946, twenty-six per cent of Canada's exports went to Britain and twenty-eight per cent to the United States. Twenty-five years later, Canada sent only four per cent of her exports to Britain and seventy per cent to the United States. Such a dramatic shift did not occur without controversy, many Conservatives believing that the changes were bad. They argued that the Liberal Party had given Canada away to the American empire, selling our British birthright. At the end of the war, however, the US dollar reigned supreme everywhere. The pound, battered by the war and paralysed by huge debts, was weak. The British imposed many defensive restrictions on imports and foreign exchange (several of which lasted until the 1970s). Had Ottawa not encouraged Canadian companies to sell more in the United States, Canada would have been in financial difficulties too. But the larger reason for the shift in our trade was that Britain was no longer so important a trading nation; Canada had little option but to look elsewhere to boost its exports. There was only one alternative: to become a poorer, weaker, financially unstable country, more — not less — dependent on the United States. As Howe put it, "Nothing is as dependent as a bankrupt."

By the 1950s, the United States had become so large and prosperous that it increasingly looked to Canada for many resources American producers could no longer supply. The two countries, then, needed each other. Each was the other's best customer and chief supplier.

It is a truism that most countries stand four-square for freer trade but show marked reluctance to follow through on their pledges when it is their own domestic markets that are to be opened to world competition. So it is that further agreements under GATT have always been the result of long, hard bargaining. In 1963 new negotiations to lower tariffs, the Kennedy Round, got under way.

The Liberal government entered the talks with mixed feelings. It wanted the opportunity to get more of its exports into world markets, particularly the increasingly protectionist European Community. But if it conceded too much in return, it would jeopardize Canadian manufacturing industries. The proposal that the United States had put on the table was for a fifty per cent across-the-board tariff cut. On the face of it, this appeared to be a proposition that every right-thinking free trader could support. But on closer examination, Canada would lose a great deal more than she gained. A large proportion of Canadian exports, then as now, was of raw materials — products on which other countries' tariffs were already low or non-existent. Many of her imports, conversely, were manufactured goods. A sharply reduced tariff could have a devastating effect on Canadian manufacturing.

At the beginning of the talks, Canada's special status as a major exporter of natural resources was recognized and concessions made. This increased Canada's bargaining power when it came time to offer concessions of our own. The eventual agreement called for significant reductions in the US tariff for both resources and manufactured products. The European Community lowered its tariff on a range of Canadian goods by about one-third. In return, Canada removed some of the bricks from the top of her own tariff wall for a range of manufactured imports (although not for textiles, a sector in which we maintained substantial protection). All the agreed changes would be introduced gradually so that industry could adjust to new competition and anticipate new export opportunities. At home, the government announced a programme of assistance to those industries adversely affected by the reduced tariffs. There would also be assistance to help companies catch the scent of new export markets. When the talks were successfully concluded in 1967, Robert Winters, the Minister of Trade and Commerce who headed the Canadian delegation, was in no doubt that the final agreement was a good one for Canada. "The success of the Kennedy Round," he said, "has wide-ranging implications, opening new, broad perspectives of expanded trade and benefitting all sectors and regions of the economy."

The pursuit of trade liberalization was the cornerstone of trade policy during the 1960s and 1970s. In the long run, Canadian consumers would benefit from fresh competition. Canadian companies would be able to produce goods more cheaply by selling into larger markets abroad as well as at home. If industry took advantage of such export opportunities, more jobs would be created. The Kennedy Round was important in the Liberal economic strategy for another reason, too. Trade agreements involving many nations provided the best check against protectionism in emerging trading blocs. Since bilateral trade with the United States was vital, it was important to gain even greater access to American markets. This the Kennedy Round offered.

Relations with the United States will always, of necessity, play a dominant role in Canada's affairs, no matter what party is in power. Since the War of 1812, Canada and the United States have gradually forged the diplomatic tools to make feasible the sharing of a continent. To manage the many problems which have inevitably arisen since the Second World War, Liberal governments have constructed with the Americans an intricate web of committees, joint boards and various informed diplomatic ties.

Such special relations with the United States developed over decades. Given the proximity and relative strength of the two nations, Ottawa never had any alternative but to work out as advantageous a deal as it could. Every government since Laurier's has known this. Perhaps in theory there is an alternative of sorts, but diplomatic hardball could only have ended in unstable and dangerous retaliation; a cold war along the Forty-ninth Parallel would have left Canada the clear loser.

Another theoretical extreme was some form of free trade area or even a commercial union with the United States. But bilateral (as distinct from global) free trade would have undermined Canada's sovereignty, compromising our ability to build a different nation with different values from those of our southern neighbour. The Liberal approach to the US-Canadian relationship has rejected both these alternatives. The bedrock of Liberal strategy was preservation of our national interests and independence, along with strengthening our own economy by increased US trade. The best way to benefit from our powerful neighbour had been to perfect bilateral tools to give Canada greater bargaining power.

Of course, as with any special relationship, there has not always been smooth sailing. In the 1960s, Canada felt with some force the discomfort of being the weaker power — of being, as the saying goes, in bed with an elephant. During this period Washington became increasingly concerned at the massive outflows of US dollars and in 1963 imposed an "interest equalization tax," making it more expensive for foreigners to borrow in the United States. Since Canadian companies and many of the provinces borrowed heavily in the States, the change would have had a serious effect on Canadian balance of payments. It was estimated that the regulation would have added at least one percentage point to the cost of raising money in US markets. Similar crises were to occur in 1965 and 1968.

A succession of Liberal ministers hastened to Washington to plead, usually with success, for Canadian exemption. The government really had no other choice. US restrictions could affect the stability of the Canadian dollar and threaten the foundations of the Canadian economy — as actually happened during the 1969 crisis. These facts were not to the liking of those who saw in this just how dependent Canada had become. But it is difficult to see what alternative the government had. In any event, our success in winning exemption from the restrictions was a sign of just how strong the special relations between the two countries had grown.

Another, and still more controversial side of the Liberal management of Canadian-US relations was the Auto Pact of 1965. By the 1960s, it was clear that the US-dominated automobile industry in Canada was doomed unless it could win access to the entire North American market. Towering new tariff walls might have kept the industry afloat but only at an enormous cost to the consumer. In markets where imports from Japan and Europe were still few, manufacturing in Canada would share in the increase in US production and sales. A web of supply companies had also developed on both sides of the border. Given that structure, it made economic sense to look for greater efficiencies there too. In 1963, Canada tried by an export incentive scheme to boost its car exports. But this was a stop-gap measure, especially since it invited retaliation abroad in the form of countervailing duties. The Auto Pack offered a better solution. Under the agreement, Washington eliminated tariffs on imports by American auto companies of cars and parts made in Canada. In return, Canada removed restrictions on the import of cars and parts by companies in Canada, provided that a specified level of Canadian work went into the cars and that the ratio of car production and car sales in Canada was met. The Liberal government established a loan assistance programme for companies which might suffer during the industry's rationalization and provided supplemental unemployment insurance benefits for employees. Canada did well by the Auto Pact for many years, so well, in fact, that in the early 1970s the US government was upset by the amount of auto imports from Canada. Later, the auto industry throughout North America was rocked by high fuel costs and cheaper, more fuel-efficient imported cars. Quotas on imported automobiles gave only temporary shelter as the industry regrouped to modernize and to produce what the customer clearly sought.

39

There is no question that in the expansionary period of the 1950s and 1960s, Liberal trade policies had worked. The 1970s, however, brought new challenges. The adverse US balance of trade, exacerbated by that country's massive spending on the Vietnam War, combined to threaten the stability of the international economic system so painstakingly built since the war. In 1971, therefore, President Richard Nixon imposed sweeping measures aimed at reducing the flow of capital from his country. Canada, which sometimes in the past had run up large trade surpluses with the United States, was not exempt this time. Once again our Finance Minister travelled to Washington, but unlike in 1963 and 1968 was greeted by a tough, inflexible stance. To disconcerted Canadian officials, the American response this time seemed to violate the postwar practices of negotiation and compromise.

With traditional methods proving ineffective, Ottawa announced assistance for the adversely affected Canadian companies. It was obvious, however, that a more far-reaching settlement of grievances would have to be found. Finance Minister Edgar Benson chaired a meeting of the IMF principal trading nations which agreed on a new alignment of currencies. The United States then removed its import tax surcharge and certain other provisions obnoxious to its trading partners. In retrospect, the chilly tone in Canadian-US relations during the early 1970s had much to do with the need for a larger adjustment in the postwar economic order to take account of the growing power of Europe and Japan.

The tough US attitude towards Canada sent a shock wave through the Liberal government. Would the traditional tools of Canadian-American diplomacy continue to work as they had in the past? Perhaps the time had come for a re-examination of Canada's trade policies. In 1972, therefore, the government published its White Paper on Canada-US Relations. In essence the White Paper offered three options. The first two were to maintain the status quo or to move towards still greater integration with the US. Both these two were rejected. The third option defined the national interest in a tougher way and urged a stronger sense of strategy when Canada sat down to bargain with the United States and the world.

One goal of this Third Option, as it came to be called, was to "create a sounder, less vulnerable economic base for competing in the domestic and world markets and deliberately to broaden the spectrum of markets in which Canadians can and will compete." In this there was a reaffirmation of earlier Liberal policy. Since 1944, successive governments had done everything they could to make sure the world, not just the United States, was more accessible to Canadian exports. That is why the Liberals, led by St. Laurent and Pearson, had placed so much importance on the creation of the IMF and of GATT. In the 1960s, the government set out even more energetically to promote Canadian sales abroad. The Third Option may have refurbished some old themes in Liberal trade strategy, but they were to be acted upon with a greater sense of urgency. In the 1970s, the government orchestrated an even more vigorous strategy of export promotion in Europe, the Pacific and Latin America. In 1976 Canada signed a "contractual link" with the European Community as a base for expanding economic relations; new trade agreements and committees opened doors into many other countries.

One prime objective of the Third Option was to help redress the balance of our extensive ties with the United States. Also, the government realized that the Canadian-American relationship itself had to be revised. The practices of compromise and negotiation must be maintained, but Canada's interests had to be asserted with more clarity and force. The Americans were proving to be increasingly tough bargainers. Canada had to respond in kind. Allan MacEachen, the Secretary of State for External Affairs in the late 1970s (and again in the 1980s), welcomed this frank tone. "It will bring with it new difficulties, especially when the Canadian and American perceptions over an issue do not run parallel," he said, "but the state of dynamic tension is a healthy one."

By 1974, some of the irritants which had plagued relations during Richard Nixon's administration were removed (along with Nixon himself who resigned that year). With the election of President Jimmy Carter in 1976, the relationship seemed to right itself. But some of our policies — petroleum regulation, agricultural quotas and foreign investment review — rankled Washington. On our side, there were complaints about the Auto Pact, the extension of US law to the operations of American subsidiaries in Canada and the negotiation of a new fisheries treaty. To these were added contentious environmental issues, primarily the Garrison Division Project, Great Lakes pollution and acid rain. "Quiet diplomacy" had to become noisier. A telephone call to the White House or a visit to the State Department no longer seemed enough. To influence Congress, more aggressive lobbying was necessary. At times Canada had to appeal directly to the American public, over the head of politicians; the acid rain issue is an example. Nevertheless the list of disputes has grown, especially during the international recession. President Ronald Reagan's administration has taken tough stands on what it sees as US interests. Canada has won on some issues, lost on others. The tradition of compromise, remains.

Preoccupied as all Canadian governments have been (some would say mesmerized) with relations with the United States, it is easy to ignore changes taking place elsewhere. Sometimes, however, events force themselves on our attention. For example, the 1973 oil crisis and problems flowing from it have concentrated Canadian minds wonderfully on the interdependence of the world's economies. As the world stage became more crowded with nations rapidly industrializing, Liberals realized how important it has become to improve

41

international institutions. Quite early on Ottawa set out to exploit possible opportunities to influence international economic institutions. For example, John Turner, as Minister of Finance, chaired a committee to reform the IMF. From its recommendations emerged a more flexible institution, better suited to new challenges, including the cushioning of the impact of international recession.

Since the end of the Second World War Canada has looked beyond its traditional horizons to the problems and concerns of the Third World. During the 1950s, we sponsored new nations as members of the UN, occasionally against the will of the great powers. As a leading member of the evolving Commonwealth, we championed its Colombo Plan, a pioneering model for aiding poorer nations. Direct assistance to help alleviate poverty, hunger and illiteracy became a Liberal commitment. Most of the credit for the initiatives taken must go to Lester Pearson and to Paul Martin: the strong, internationalist and compassionate conscience they shared deeply influenced the party and gave Canada a leading role in the development of international assistance, in terms of both aid and trade. Trudeau shared their commitment, increasing Canada's contributions during the 1970s. Trade, it was increasingly obvious, was an essential key to Third World development. In the United Nations, in the GATT and in other international economic gatherings, Canada supported the movement for liberalization of trade between the industrial and the developing nations. The net of postwar economic institutions — the World Bank, the IMF and GATT — had to be cast further to take account of the Third World's particular problems. But progress has remained slow. Yet in the party today, the Pearson commitment to developing countries remains strong.

THE LIBERALS
AND ECONOMIC POLICY

The Liberal Party King bequeathed to St. Laurent was well prepared for the transition to a peacetime economy. In the turbulent period following the First World War the Union Party under Sir Robert Borden had stumbled and finally collapsed. That would not happen to the Liberals. Even before the Second World War ended they were planning for the future. The 1945 White Paper on Employment and Income was the master plan for postwar prosperity. By any reckoning, it worked. Investment poured into factories and resource industries and the Gross National Product shot upward. Canadians had more to invest and more to spend than ever before.

C.D. Howe was justified in his conviction that prosperity was the best form of social security. As an engineer and businessman, Howe firmly believed that the federal government must provide the national leadership to create a climate of stability and confidence but at the same time avoid burdening the taxpayers by giving subsidies to inefficient and unprofitable industries. A tested veteran of wartime economic management, he knew how business worked. He shared its codes and customs, including the conviction that profits fuelled economic growth through further investment.

In 1945 Mackenzie King had explained that "the largest part of the employment required must be provided by private undertaking." But he went to say that "in certain fields, the public interest calls for public enterprise in national development. In those fields, we have not, and, in the future, will not hesitate, in the general interest to promote bold action by the state." Such was the broad policy of active government involvement about which Howe observed, "If our national development had been left entirely to private enterprise, Canada would not have attained its present status as a nation. And unless government continues to take a lead by well-planned initiatives, guidance and regulation, it will not develop as it should."

So after the war Howe alternatively prodded and cajoled businesses with tax breaks and assistance into finding new markets. A favourite device — one which reached a high level of sophistication in Canada — was the crown corporation. Many companies producing strategic material during the war had been under Howe's direct control. Now they assumed an identity of their own, at arm's length from the government: Polymer in the synthetic rubber industry, Eldorado and later AECL in the small but growing nuclear energy industry, and Howe's own favourite, Trans-Canada Air Lines. Run like businesses, they gave the national government direct involvement in the success of Canadian enterprise. There were also the "big projects," at least one of which Howe liked to have under way at any given time. The St. Lawrence Seaway, a joint Canada-US undertaking, finally opened a modernized water corridor into the industrial heartland of North America, largely as a result of persistent Canadian initiative. Also the Trans-Canada Pipeline was constructed to carry natural gas from Western Canada to Ontario. From the Liberal government's point of view, the big projects of the 1950s did more than just boost employment and stimulate industry; they created a national sense of confidence, enterprise and success. These were leading elements of Liberal economic policy during the St. Laurent era.

The Liberal government used its national authority during the 1950s to manage the economy and to keep it firmly on the path to prosperity. It used tools originally designed by Keynes and forged during and immediately following the war. In a market economy like Canada's, government could use its spending power and influence on monetary policy either to stimulate or to restrain economic growth. These options were like the pedals of a car. A touch on the accelerator would speed up the economy, a touch on the brake slow it. With demand for Canadian products increasing, Ottawa had the opportunity to steer the nation along the middle road between inflation and unemployment. St. Laurent's Finance Ministers, first Douglas Abbott and then Walter Harris, understood this perfectly well and, joined by Howe, skilfully managed the economy throughout the decade. At home and abroad, the Liberal government won an enviable reputation for its competence in economic management. *The Economist* summed up international opinion: "Canada's economic affairs have been handled with a skill unexampled throughout the world."

This achievement would have been remarkable in a unitary state. It was all the more so under a federal system of government. It seems to be in the nature of things that the various levels of government in a federation are in a state of more or less permanent confrontation. For the system to function satisfactorily a large measure of compromise is essential. This the Liberal Party has always understood.

The foundation of our federal system is as much economic as it is political, which is why much federal-provincial wrangling has taken place over money. Fiscal policy and tax-sharing probably rank with the tariff as among the least inspiring subjects for the general reader. Yet, like the tariff, they have constantly occupied a pivotal role in Canadian affairs.

The terms of Confederation granted to the provinces the right to raise direct taxes for provincial purposes. Those being the days before income tax, this was understood to mean revenue from property taxes, customs duties, licence fees, etc. Income tax was introduced by the federal government as a temporary measure during the First World War. Because of the huge war debt later, it was not removed.

During the Depression the provinces entered into the income and corporation tax field themselves in an effort to make provincial ends meet.

With the start of the Second World War, the provinces were persuaded to surrender their taxing powers to the federal government, to finance the national war effort. But after the war, as we have seen, they sought to regain the power to raise their own taxes. The Liberals under King were loath to go back to the fiscal chaos of the 1930s. Their view was put clearly in the 1947 budget speech by Minister of Finance J.L. Ilsley. "This problem is far more than one of taxation alone," he said. "What is at stake is Canada's ability to have an effective antidepression policy and to maintain full employment and a high national income after the present abnormal transition period is over; and to achieve a reasonable standard of economic security for all Canadians no matter in what part of the country they may live."

With these objectives always in mind, successive Liberal governments have bargained with the provinces over how to divide the nation's financial resources. In 1947, under the tax rental agreements, any province agreeing not to levy its own income and corporation taxes would be given a share of federal tax revenues. All the provinces agreed, except Ontario and Quebec, and even they did not introduce their own taxes, not right away at least. In 1954 Premier Maurice Duplessis of Quebec did introduce a separate provincial income tax. St. Laurent, always the patient conciliator, patched up an agreement with Duplessis allowing uniformity in taxation. While it lasted, the taxing crisis had served to illustrate the continuing fragility of the financial underpinnings of Confederation.

If the postwar tax-sharing scheme unravelled, Confederation itself might follow. Both stability and equity had to be reflected in the fiscal arrangements of Confederation. So in 1956 St. Laurent offered a new, strikingly innovative tax proposal, promising a high degree of financial stability for both the federal and provincial governments. The new agreement was a major revolution in the way Confederation was to work. Each province would be awarded tax points, to be "equalized" between the richest and the poorest provinces.

St. Laurent's federal-provincial tax-sharing proposal was, in a sense, his own National Policy in what was perhaps the last great frontier: creative governing to improve the security, welfare and prosperity of Canadians from one end of the country to the other. A succession of Liberal governments have been willing to make "fiscal room" for the provinces, so that the several provincial governments could impose their own taxes and spend them as they wished. Ottawa stopped taxing estates. It dramatically reduced its rates of personal income tax. It perfected a system of "equalization" grants, through which the have-not provinces received large unconditional grants

45

which they could spend however they chose. But this 1950s and early 1960s prosperity had been bought at a price which some people, especially the NDP, considered too high. Much of the investment and entrepreneurial skills that had built the Canadian economy had come from abroad, particularly from the United States. By the mid-1960s, our industry had more capacity and we more confidence in Canadian sources; foreign ownership became the big issue.

When the Liberals defeated the Conservative government in 1963, the incoming Pearson administration contained many new faces, among them the new Minister of Finance, Walter Gordon. "For some time during the late 1940s and early 1950s," Gordon would recall in his memoirs, "I had been worrying about the government's economic policies, and particularly the complacency with which Canadians were witnessing the sell-out of our resources and business enterprises to Americans and other enterprising foreigners." Howe had stressed that foreign-owned businesses must conform to Canada's broader interests. He was confident that they would; Gordon was not so sure. In the report of the Royal Commission on Canada's Economic Prospects in 1957 (presented to the Diefenbaker government), Gordon had warned of the dangers pervasive foreign investment posed for national sovereignty. By the late 1950s, economic nationalism had become the central theme of his public life. A skilful wartime public servant and highly respected Toronto businessman, Gordon carried these concerns into the heart of the Liberal Party. As Finance Minister, he brought down a budget which included a controversial tax on foreign takeovers and measures to encourage greater Canadian ownership and control. There were technical problems in these nationalistic proposals and, under heavy fire, they were withdrawn. For the moment, at least, it seemed that Gordon was too far ahead of the party and the people. Undiscouraged, he set out on a long, patient campaign, frequently in the face of hostility from the business community and provincial governments.

After the 1965 election, Gordon left the cabinet and was succeeded at Finance by Mitchell Sharp who brought a more traditional approach to the growing debate about foreign investment. Sharp had been one of the young, bright lights in Howe's Department of Trade and Commerce during the St. Laurent years, but when Diefenbaker came along was frozen out. He became one of Pearson's new Liberals and, before moving to the Finance portfolio, served as Trade and Commerce Minister.

In many broad respects, Sharp carried on the Howe tradition of economic management. Within the party in the 1960s, he and Gordon came to symbolize the two largely divergent views on the issue of economic nationalism. Not surprisingly, the growing debate was carried into the party conventions and into cabinet itself.

From the distance of twenty and more years, we can see that the

St. Laurent and Howe Liberals were not, as some economic national-
ists today would have it, continentalists. True, in 1957 Howe had
dismissed Gordon's report as so much nonsense. But Howe too thought
of himself as an economic nationalist, believing that the best way for
Canada to become a strong, independent nation was to use foreign
investment to help build its economy. In his view, the alternative was a
slower rate of growth, less prosperity and a weaker, more vulnerable
and dependent nation. For now, foreign enterprise and foreign capital
were useful tools to promote economic growth. Reliance on them
would naturally lessen as the economy grew. Sharp was an economic
nationalist in much the same way. There were all sorts of things that
government might do to encourage Canadians to invest and to enforce
good corporate citizenship on foreign companies and investors. But
discouraging outside investment by more forceful means would, Sharp
was convinced, quickly slow down and damage our increasing
prosperity. These opposing conceptions of the national interest and the
impact of foreign investment contended within the party throughout
the late 1960s.

By the 1970s, there was increasing concern in Canada, as in many
other countries, about multinational companies. Many Liberals worried that the high degree of American ownership and heavy reliance
on US markets were cramping our ability to pursue an independent
foreign policy and to realize our national economic interests. As a
partial answer to this, in 1972 the government set up the Canada
Development Corporation (Gordon's brainchild) to manage a portfolio of crown corporations and to invest in Canadian companies. The
CDC, although it served a political purpose, was to be managed like a
business. Herb Gray, the most persistent proponent of Gordon's concerns within the Trudeau cabinet, produced a second major report on
the foreign control issue. As a result, the Foreign Investment Review
Agency (FIRA) was created to screen takeovers and new acquisitions by
foreign-owned companies already operating in Canada. FIRA demanded
proof that any proposal brought substantial benefits and was clearly in
the national interest. These instruments of economic nationalism did
not go far enough for some Liberals while for others they went too far.
In a sense, FIRA was a moderate, practical compromise between these
contending views.

In the 1950s and 1960s, the Liberal Party had watched over and
finetuned one of the world's most prosperous economies. During the
1970s, however, the engine of economic growth began to sputter. The
basic problem was inflation. Buoyant private investment had kept
demand and employment high in the period up to 1957. There was
more inflation than one might have hoped for, but it would have been
hard for Canada, with her worldwide trading needs, to "opt out" of
an inflationary process that was global.

The record in the 1960s and 1970s was more mixed than in the

47

years before 1957, but at least living standards were still rising. The Pearson and Trudeau governments made serious efforts, through tax policy and controls on their own spending, to stimulate the right sorts of economic activity and to restrain inflation. Also, the government and the Bank of Canada worked together to control the level of monetary growth. The government's task was more difficult because, as we shall see in the next chapter, so many of the new and expanded social programmes involved open-ended commitments to spending. Other outlays — for instance, on defence and on the civil service itself — were rigidly controlled. For more than a decade the number of federal officials did not increase, though the work load of the federal government grew rapidly.

By the late 1960s, in Canada as in other countries, many observers believed that an inflationary psychology was becoming entrenched, and that new devices would have to be tried if inflation was to be reduced. The government learned partly from the experience of other countries. First it established a consultative Prices and Incomes Commission. Then it created a body to monitor consumer pricing practices. Eventually, from 1975-7, it experimented with direct controls over prices and wages. This last step was contrary to the general thrust of Liberal thinking since 1945. It was also contrary to the previously expressed intention of the Trudeau government. But it was justified at the time to break the inflationary psychology and to supplement the more traditional management of fiscal and monetary policy. The only alternative would have been sweeping cuts in money, credit, and government spending, or painful increases in taxation rates. In 1982, the government introduced a rigorous policy of wage-control in the public service (the "six and five" programme). Other employers followed its example.

In judging the Liberal government's economic management record after 1963, we should recall that the record of other governments was much the same: accelerating inflation between the mid-1960s and the late 1970s, some disillusionment with fiscal policy and monetary policy, and a tendency to experiment with direct controls for longer or shorter periods. Inflation was a worldwide phenomenon from which Canada could not readily have opted out, although many economists believe that government policies might have been more finely tuned. Certainly Ottawa was willing to learn from others and to experiment. But the policies of the years from 1945 to 1957 had become harder to implement, with the provinces now accounting for a much larger share of taxing and spending. Moreover, it was thought that opposition to tax increases had grown. Also, many of the joint programmes could not readily be redesigned or cut back, certainly not by Ottawa alone.

It should be emphasized that throughout the 1970s, the party did not waver in its support of social security and welfare. Social programmes were not dismantled when times got tough. Indeed, it was just in those circumstances that several had to be expanded. Pensions and allowances were increased and tied to the cost of living. The cost of unemployment insurance increased sharply, but maintaining the income of the unemployed was a social obligation not to be compromised. The indexed personal tax exemption (introduced in 1973) protected Canadians from the most insidious effect of inflation.

Canadians understand a commitment to social justice. Less well understood is the fact that the expenditures giving meaning to this commitment take a large percentage of Ottawa's total financial resources. The costs of social programmes naturally increase in periods of inflation or unemployment. When both negative economic conditions are present together, the problem is that much greater because in hard times government tax revenue also goes down. One result has been that, in recent years, the federal government has run larger deficits than it would have liked, having to borrow more to meet its obligations. Governments elsewhere, whatever their political stripe, have found themselves in much the same boat. Measured against the size of our economy, set against our past, and compared to some of our competitors in the industrial world, our national debt — what we owe against our borrowing to meet expenditures — is a necessary element in our economic recovery.

Few issues in the 1970s posed a greater challenge than the global energy crisis. In Canada, the Pearson government inherited an arrangement by which Alberta oil supplied most of Ontario while lower-cost imported oil supplied Quebec and the Atlantic provinces. When OPEC dramatically raised world prices in 1973, the Trudeau government responded by controlling domestic oil prices, subsidizing crude oil imports, and taxing exports to the United States. These measures were meant to equalize the impact of the new world prices, so that the various regions would not gain or lose unduly. As time passed, various additional measures were taken. There were conservation plans, development of additional oil sources including the tar sands, and a gradual upward movement of consumer prices, so as to reduce imports and move back to self-sufficiency in oil.

In 1980, the Liberal government launched the National Energy Programme (NEP). Under this scheme domestic crude oil prices would be increased over time to bring them up to about seventy-five per cent of the world price. A "blended" price was devised to encourage production from more expensive and new sources, especially northern and offshore. With these proposals came a more equitable division of the revenue among the industry, the producing provinces and the national government.

More dramatic and nationalistic were ideas for increased Canadianization. Under the NEP's Petroleum Incentives Programme companies would be offered grants for exploration, according to the

49

degree of Canadian ownership. Changes in the leasing of lands also favoured Canadian companies. For decades, the multinationals had been the backbone of exploration and production in Canada. During the 1970s, however, a few Canadian names appeared among the more enterprising and successful companies. The trend, however, was still slow, and accelerated Canadianization, it was reasoned, could help increase competition and speed exploration.

Concurrently, the government-owned Petrocan would be expanded; in an industry dominated by the multinationals, it would be the symbol of the national interest, an agent in the Canadianization process, an additional spur to exploration and production in the frontier areas.

What no one had anticipated, however, was the degree to which both oil consumption and its international price would fall in 1983 as OPEC underwent increasingly severe internal strains. As a result, many of Canada's energy megaprojects, especially in oil sands, were placed on the back burner. Some companies, with ambitious plans for the future, found themselves in difficulty with slower demand, higher interest rates and lower international oil prices. Changes have been made to adjust to these new conditions, but greater Canadian participation in the further development of our own energy resources will continue to be a Liberal goal.

Honed on Depression and wartime requirements, Liberal governments have tended to expand Ottawa's role in promoting economic development. Whatever the occasion, the reason has remained basically the same: Liberals believe that underlying the regions of Canada there is one national economy, one national community for the goods and services Canadians produce and buy. For Liberals, private enterprise is the basic engine of prosperity. But the federal government must act in partnership with business and labour to plan national economic growth.

Partly in response to suggestions from the business community, partly to encourage entrepreneurship, Liberal governments, especially during the past decade, have made Ottawa a sort of service centre for business, offering export promotion, technical and information services, small business loans, incentives for research and development and regional industrial expansion. In addition, Liberal governments have offered special assistance to companies to help them ride out recessions and retool for the more competitive markets ahead. For example, Canada has had a long and consistent record of encouraging the communications industry, going back to support for Marconi's early trans-Atlantic broadcasts. More recently, development grants to the telecommunications sector have helped to develop an internationally respected industry. The service centre role of the national government has evolved as a progression of pragmatic and individual responses to the needs of the economy.

So too has the crown corporation. Long a familiar feature of the Canadian economic landscape, crown corporations (whether national or provincial) have proven to be useful tools to promote development. The Canadian Broadcasting Corporation, the Bank of Canada, Air Canada and PetroCanada are among more recent federal government-owned or supported enterprises playing a vital role in transcending the limits of private investment in a vast, frequently hostile and sparsely populated terrain. It is, in fact, difficult to conceive of a Canada without both private and public entrepreneurship.

The willingness of Canadians to turn to some form of state enterprise to get done a job that cannot be done by private investors is the substantiation of Jack Pickersgill's advice to one young Liberal: "Don't play the game of whether private enterprise or public enterprise is superior. Canadians are in favour of enterprise, period."

More could be written about the many creative innovations in economic policy which ornament the years of Liberal government since 1945. No one would claim that everything has gone perfectly or that nothing could have gone better. But in economic matters the party record is one of sensible, innovative management, responsive to the wishes of the people and sensitive to their needs and concerns. Thanks to the social welfare programmes which are largely the work of Liberal governments and which we shall discuss in the next chapter, life is better for many of Canada's peoples in many regions and provinces. Thanks to the favourable environment for business investment which the party fostered, citizens are much better off than they were at the end of the Second World War. Thanks to the party's creative and imaginative leadership on the world economic scene, our foreign trade has developed apace. There have been problems, especially the inflation and unemployment of the 1970s and the cyclical downturn of 1982-83. But most Canadians live better, and all Canadians live more securely, than they did even a generation ago. In the uncertain world of the late twentieth century, that is a major achievement.

A GLORIOUS PROSPECT.

THE AULD WOMAN.—"TRULY, AS YOU SAY, SIR, THE PASTURE IS VERA POOR, BUT THE COW HAS A GRAND VIEW!"

In a style of political cartooning considered savage at the time, J.W. Bengough, a Toronto reformer, attacks Sir John A. Macdonald in 1882. The message was that although Macdonald's tariffs protected some manufacturers in Canada, they were of little or no direct help to the workers themselves.

Sir Wilfrid Laurier (shown here in 1911 in the waning days of his government) was the consummate politician and the ultimate Liberal of his time. He throve on debate and mastered the flexibility and love of compromise so essential to the consensus idea. *(Public Archives of Canada)*

The incredible (and incredibly misunderstood) Mackenzie King making a radio broadcast on May 8, 1945 — VE Day, signalling the end of the Second World War in the European Theatre. He was in San Francisco at the time for the founding conference of the United Nations. Canada's UN commitment was put to the test in 1950 when the cabinet, returning by train to Ottawa from King's funeral in Toronto, decided to join the war in Korea. *(Public Archives of Canada)*

At the Liberal leadership convention of 1948, Louis St. Laurent confers with Mackenzie King, whom he would succeed as leader and as prime minister. One of St. Laurent's most important achievements was the 1956 tax formula with its built-in equalization scheme giving financial stability to both Ottawa and the provinces. It may sound less dramatic than building a railway or putting down a rebellion, but the plan was a revolution in the way Confederation was to work. *(Public Archives of Canada)*

The eve of another turning point for the Liberal Party and for Canada. The scene is a federal-provincial constitutional conference in February 1968. Within weeks Minister of Justice Pierre Elliott Trudeau would be party leader following the retirement of his mentor Lester B. Pearson. Left background is a soon-to-be familiar face: Marc Lalonde, who would be at various times the Minister of Finance and the Minister of Energy in the Trudeau government. *(Public Archives of Canada)*

The author with John Turner shortly after Turner's selection as party leader.

LIBERAL
SOCIAL PROMISES FULFILLED

Economic policies, then, and social policies should now move forward together, and they are too often treated as separate and even conflicting. To enlarge opportunities, to improve the ability of people to take advantage of these opportunities is not only to attack poverty; it is to strengthen our whole economy, to increase the prosperity and raise the standards of the whole community.

Speech from the Throne, 1965

There are many ways in which a country can be judged. Articles appear constantly in popular journals rating countries by their economic growth, their political stability, their influence in the world. But one of the most important measures of any country must be the way in which it enhances its citizens' quality of life and cares for its disadvantaged: the young, the old, the sick, the disabled, the minorities. In any scale of values in these areas, Canada would place close to the top. It is an achievement of which all can be proud. For if Canada has had governments with the policies and the will to put in place a compassionate social system, it has also had an electorate prepared to support the cost of such a system.

This achievement has been all the more remarkable considering the nature of the Canadian federation. When the Fathers of Confederation were laying down the basis for our constitution — a basis still in place following the patriation of the British North America Act and our new Charter of Rights — they cast anxious eyes south of the border. They saw only too clearly how the power of the individual states in the United States had led to discord and an incredibly bloody civil war. Canadian politicians, Macdonald in particular, were convinced that if a federal system was to work in Canada a strong central government was essential. Therefore, under the terms of Confederation, most of the vital powers were to be left in the hands of the federal government; the provinces would have jurisdiction over only the regional, relatively unimportant areas of administration.

It is a comment on both the rural and scattered nature of Canadian society in the nineteenth century and its *laissez-faire* attitudes that the provinces were given responsibility for such "unimportant" areas as public health and education. Matters such as protection against sickness, unemployment, poverty and old age were hardly considered, the assumption being that such things were best left to private charity.

Public attitudes have since changed. The miseries of the Depression did away with any such simplistic reliance on private charity.

59

Never again would the state be able to stand aside and allow widespread poverty and economic hardship to take their course.

The Liberal Party, in understanding this, was ready at the end of the Second World War with a plan for social security. The Green Book of 1945 enunciated clearly the path the national government intended to take. But Ottawa had to move cautiously. As we have seen, the provinces, having given up much of their taxing powers to Ottawa for the duration of the war, were anxious to regain them. In 1956 St. Laurent offered a new, strikingly innovative tax proposal with a built-in equalization formula promising a high degree of financial stability for both the federal and provincial governments. The new agreement was a major revolution in the way Confederation was to work.

Despite this tax-sharing success, however, any attempt by Ottawa to impose its social legislation in matters of provincial concern would continue to be met with vigorous opposition. There were those, too, in the Liberal Party who advocated caution. The dislocation and the economic problems following the First World War made them chary of plunging into too many expensive social programmes.

So the Liberal dream of social security for all Canadians would not come wholly true until the balmy 1960s. By then, a conjunction of circumstances led to a flurry of necessary legislation. The economy was booming, unemployment was falling, and there seemed no such thing as limits to growth. This in turn led to a climate of opinion, fuelled by the enthusiastic media, that demanded reform, including a more equitable distribution of wealth. The time was ripe for large schemes designed to place under every Canadian a "social security net." Finally, the time had come for the Liberals to honour old commitments. Stunned by its defeat in the 1958 election, the party set out to renew itself. While in opposition, it had fielded a multitude of reform ideas good and bad. Gradually a new spirit of liberalism gained ground. In 1960, a highly publicized conference at Kingston thrashed out new policies. The following year, Liberals from across the country met in Ottawa and, drawing upon the Kingston experience, committed the party to a package of progressive social policies.

So it was that, when returned to office in 1963, under Pearson's leadership, the party was ready for the challenge. When the Pearson cabinet was sworn in, it was clear that a new generaton had arrived in Ottawa. The business orientation exemplified by C.D. Howe was less conspicuous now; in its place were the more socially concerned, *dirigiste* politics of Walter Gordon and Judy LaMarsh.

The full measure of the postwar Liberal social platform become clear under Pearson during the 1960s. Pearson restored the emphasis on "positive liberalism." Classical liberalism stressed the liberty of the individual; positive liberalism recognized that the realization of individual freedom could be obstructed by the lack of opportunity. But much of the ground work had been done under St. Laurent in, for example, old age pensions. St. Laurent had recognized the inadequacy of the 1927 Old Age Pension Act and, with the willing support of the provinces for once, set about improving it. Under the new act, federal pensions became available to all Canadians over age seventy. In addition, under the Old Age Assistance Act, Ottawa shared with the provinces the costs of pensions for needy citizens between ages sixty and sixty-five. In 1951 and again in 1954, the government entered into shared-costs programmes with the provinces to help the blind and otherwise disabled.

But such expansion was not enough for the 1960s. The Liberals had fought the 1963 election with the slogan "Better Pensions for All." After their victory, Pearson, perhaps rashly, committed the party to "sixty days of decision" (Canadians then, if not now, loved to emulate Americans in slogans, as in much else). One of these decisions was to introduce a compulsory, nationwide, contributory pension plan. With the Canada Pension Plan, social security for the aged was redrawn. Now there were federal pensions for widows, orphans and the disabled. In an important departure, benefits under the plan were geared to the cost of living. There remained, however, a major stumbling block. Quebec wanted to run its own provincial scheme, being reluctant to acknowledge any national responsibility. After much shuttle diplomacy between Ottawa and Quebec City, there was an agreement that allowed the Canada Pension Plan to become law in 1965. The agreement let any province manage its own scheme, provided certain national standards were observed. To complete the new security plan for the aged, the Pearson government in 1966 introduced a Guaranteed Income Supplement, providing a minimum income for needy seniors unable to take advantage of the Canada Pension Plan and for whom the old age security pension alone was too small.

In 1973, in a move designed to offer seniors some protection from inflation, both the old age security pension and the Guaranteed Income Supplement were increased and indexed to the cost of living. These improvements cost the federal taxpayer more, but not to have introduced them would have undermined needed assistance to people who were especially vulnerable.

Next on Pearson's agenda was medicare. Again the Liberals could build on their previous programmes. As early as 1947, Ottawa had entered the health field through grants to the provinces (an indirect way of getting into what had been seen as an exclusively provincial responsibility). A decade later, the St. Laurent government took another step with the Hospital Insurance and Diagnostic Services Act, under which Ottawa offered to pay one-half the costs of hospital care, provided the provinces made the scheme available to everyone.

In 1965, flushed with victory at the passing of their pension legislation, the Liberal government again turned its attention to health

61

care. Pearson announced that his government was ready to provide, on average, one-half the cost of provincial health insurance. Millions of Canadians, especially in rural and poorer regions and those on low incomes, had little or no insurance to protect them from the sometimes ruinous costs of illness. As with other shared-cost programmes, the government demanded national standards as the major condition for its support. The provincial schemes had to be universal, insurance coverage had to be "portable" across provincial boundaries, and the plans had to be run by provincial governments, not by private entities. When agreement in principle was finally reached in 1968, medicare became the vehicle through which Canada created one of the world's most effective systems of health care. It was the national government which had initiated the insurance schemes, and Ottawa continues to support them despite the provincial label medicare now carries.

There was more to come. In the same month the Canada Pension Plan was given royal assent, Pearson announced plans for a comprehensive welfare assistance programme. As we have seen, the governments of King and St. Laurent had provided help to the aged, blind and disabled and, in 1956, Unemployment Assistance boosted provincial welfare for the jobless. In all these programmes, Ottawa and the provinces had agreed to set aside constitutional squabbles in the interest of reducing hardship. Under the new Canada Assistance Plan, these programmes would be grouped together and the benefits increased; this was a watershed in social development, providing Canadians for the first time with a comprehensive national welfare programme. There would be more federal support for improving social services for youth, native peoples, and those needing special rehabilitation to find jobs. Again, as a condition of federal support, Ottawa required the provinces to adhere to national standards. In 1967, once the details had been agreed upon with the provinces, the plan became law.

The implementation of the Canada Pension Plan and medicare underlines a fundamental principle of Confederation: an equal level of social services and equal opportunity for all Canadians, no matter where they live. This has been the philosophy of the tax-sharing programs, the tax-rental systems, the equalization payments and the cost-sharing programs which mark the path of federal-provincial relations. It is for this reason that Liberal governments have used the power of the federal purse to cajole the provinces into meeting national standards for social services. Giving a fair share of the nation's wealth to the poorer provinces has been the cornerstone of the Liberal concept of Confederation. Transfer payments under the equalization formula, and federal funding for health and social services, have worked to bring the poorer provinces up to a basic national level.

During the 1960s, the Pearson government introduced regional development policies to expand the economy of poorer areas and to

62

help create local jobs. In 1963, for example, Ottawa offered tax incentives to attract industry to those areas. These incentives were replaced in 1965 with a more ambitious scheme, the Area Development Programme, with grants tied to the amount of investment; a new formula identified the qualifying regions. From the beginning, Quebec and the four Atlantic provinces were the chief beneficiaries. Further aid came from the Atlantic Development Board which was given a broader mandate and more funds. There was also increased federal support for rural regions plagued by poverty. The Diefenbaker government had introduced the Agricultural Rehabilitation and Redevelopment Act to help poor farming areas. Pearson then greatly expanded federal assistance to help build up the infrastructure — roads, harbours, airports, etc. — of the low-income rural regions. To this programme was added FRED: the Fund for Rural Economic Development. Although regional disparities continue, they would today be worse if Pearson's governments — despite being in a minority — had not been so energetic and imaginative.

In the boom times of the 1950s and 1960s, most Canadians took their good fortune for granted. Economists constantly predicted a shorter work week and an increasing pay cheque. The leisure society was said to be just around the corner, if indeed it had not already arrived. But in so diverse and vast a country as Canada, there remained pockets of unemployment and groups who did not share in the general prosperity.

The Pearson government was aware that these regional discrepancies could not be fixed merely by increasing the transfer payments or by otherwise jiggling financial arrangements. People do not want handouts; they want an opportunity to share in the nation's growth. Above all, they want access to educational and employment opportunities. So in 1965 the government introduced the Manpower Consultative Service to research the impact of new technology on employment; this was an innovation that subsequently paid benefits. Federal funding for the construction of vocational schools rose dramatically. In 1966, under the Adult Occupational Training Act, Ottawa helped the unemployed with retraining courses. The following year, it assumed full responsibility for supporting the income of adults during retraining, gearing such allowances to income and the number of dependents. Such programmes not only assisted Canadians in acquiring more technical skills, but made sure the help went to those most in need. In 1965, federal employment services were integrated with the Unemployment Insurance Commission to link jobs with those seeking work. The manpower services of the Department of Labour were grouped in a new department, and a Manpower Mobility Programme began meeting some of the costs incurred in moving to distant jobs.

In an increasingly urban and affluent society, there were more falls for federal support of the universities, more than half of which had been founded since the Second World War, when federal funds flowed to the campuses in the form of veterans' allowances. More was required if those universities were to educate all the people required by a rapidly expanding and diversifying economy. The most urgent recommendation of the Massey Commission, created in 1949 to look into federal support for culture, called for federal assistance to universities, which were hard pressed to meet their obligations on provincial largesse alone. In 1951, Ottawa had given a pioneering shot in the arm to the universities and promised more. In 1966, the government increased its annual grant and direct aid. To give more Canadians the opportunity to attend university, a programme established in 1964 guaranteed low-cost student loans. At the 1967 Federal-Provincial Conference, Pearson offered to replace direct aid with transfer payments to provincial governments. Ottawa thus boosted its support for universities without encroaching on the primacy of the provinces. Yet Ottawa's role in financing higher education remains largely unrecognized.

The crowded statute books of the Pearson years mark one of the most productive periods in our legislative history. There would, however, be still more progress during the 1970s and new challenges in such areas as unemployment insurance. Indeed, the most important piece of Liberal social legislation in the 1970s was the sweeping overhaul of the Unemployment Insurance Commission. The 1940 act was designed basically as a social insurance vehicle; many seasonal occupations and higher income levels were excluded, and employer and employee paid equal premiums. In 1970, the Trudeau government released its White Paper on Unemployment Insurance and, following public debate, introduced a new act the following year. Henceforth the programme would be regarded more as a redistributive and income-maintenance. The old ceiling on insurable annual incomes ($2,000 in 1941 and $7,000 by 1970) was abolished and replaced by almost universal coverage for working Canadians. Many groups previously without protection were now brought in; strict eligibility requirements were eased and benefits raised. Regional patterns of unemployment were now taken fully into account in calculating how long benefits might be claimed. This was a major help to Canadians in the Atlantic provinces especially.

The new Unemployment Insurance Commission meant that the jobless could now maintain themselves at a higher percentage of their working income.

The Liberal Party early on recognized the impact that an aging population would have in our economic and social structure during the last decades of this century. Thus its determination to help the elderly was not only tradition but foresight. The party tripled family allowances, and gave them some immunity from inflation. Thereafter family allowances were treated as taxable income, so that most of the

64

benefit of the increase went to lower-income families. One more step was taken in 1978 with the Child Tax Credit. Under this scheme, tax credits would be largest for low-income families.

During the 1960s, the Pearson Liberals had built large, flexible national programmes in social security. During the next decade, attention shifted to the problems of how to fund and manage them. Mackenzie King had stayed clear of providing the provinces with federal grants, fearing that Parliament would have little control over the spending. But after the Second World War, Ottawa and the provinces had found in the shared-cost solution a way to reconcile the national interest with provincial responsibilities. During the 1970s, however, some of King's misgivings proved warranted. Under the shared-cost programmes, the federal government met much of the provincial costs, but with little or no control over the spending. By the late 1960s, the total expense was increasing dramatically. One solution was for Ottawa to get out of the programmes altogether. But that would have undermined the national interest, and hardly would have been popular with the provinces which, in some cases, had only agreed to take part in a programme by being guaranteed some form of cost-sharing. So the government eventually proposed a formula, tied to the rate of economic growth, for federal funding of higher education and health care.

Although the rapid increase in federal funding for higher education had been slowed, support for health care continued to rise (in 1974 alone it grew by twenty per cent). It was clear by 1975 that a ceiling would have to be imposed. Even after the hospital insurance agreement of 1957 had been renegotiated, federal funding would grow at well above ten per cent annually until a better system could be devised. In 1976, the Liberal government proposed a new financing arrangement with the provinces, and after the pot was sweetened with more concessions, a new agreement was finally struck.

The provinces had become more obstinate and by the mid-1970s the desire for a further push in social welfare seemed to lessen. Marc Lalonde and Monique Begin, as ministers of Health and Welfare in the 1970s and 1980s, tried to stimulate discussion of possible innovations. Their proposals included simplification of the existing schemes through a minimum guaranteed annual income which in essence would have consolidated existing practices. But most of the wide-ranging suggestions in Lalonde's 1973 Working Paper on Social Security were not enacted due to provincial reluctance and the fear, especially in the business community, that welfare programmes interfered with economic growth. There is, however, strong public support for the basic elements of the welfare system, and any government threatening to remove the underpinnings of the extensive welfare structure would do so at its peril.

With the coming of the 1970s, the oil crisis and undeniable signs of an economic slowdown, the momentum for reform diminished. By then Liberal reformers had permanently altered Canada's social and economic fabric in a compassionate way; the national picture was in stark contrast to the bleak, individualist landscape of the 1930s. Even at the height of the recession of the 1980s, there was no thought of dismantling the social service system.

THE LIBERAL PARTY
AND WORLD AFFAIRS

We have seen how Canada emerged from the Second World War a fully independent nation, ready to appear on the global stage in her own right. But if the war had taught the Allies anything it was that isolationism was no longer a tenable policy; that the world had become interdependent and that, accordingly, the rule of law and international security should be every nation's business.

Canada therefore played a prominent role in the building of postwar international organizations aimed at world stability: the United Nations, the International Monetary Fund, the World Bank. Canada also helped to create the Western alliance or, more specifically, the North Atlantic Treaty Organization (NATO). As the Iron Curtain clanked down across Europe, the hostility of Soviet policies, especially in Eastern Europe, became more obvious. Liberal foreign policy placed Canada firmly on the side of a strong NATO. Pearson in 1949, then Secretary of State for External Affairs, posed the situation in these terms.

> Foreign policy ... must be directed to one single end, the avoidance by every means within its power of atomic catastrophe. How can we do this? By burying our heads in the snow and allowing others to make the decisions without our participation, which would bind us in spite of ourselves? There is no safety there. Or relying wholly on the United Nations? That ... would be clearly unrealistic because that body ... does [not] in present circumstances provide an effective instrument for use in removing the causes of war ... The best way is for the free nations to stand together ... to make it clear that no aggressor has any possible chance of winning any war which he may be tempted to start. It is necessary to accumulate enough force now to preserve freedom in order that ultimately freedom can be preserved without force.

Canada was soon challenged to live up to those words. In 1950, communist North Korea invaded the non-communist South. For once the United Nations took firm and immediate action (the USSR had earlier walked out of the Security Council and was therefore not present to use its veto). An international force under the aegis of the UN was dispatched to halt the aggression. Canada contributed to this force, the decision having been made by the cabinet on the train carrying them back to Ottawa from Mackenzie King's funeral in Toronto.

It was rapidly becoming clear that the postwar, nuclear world was a dangerous place which demanded different policies from King's isolationist approach of the 1930s. The Korean war and the communist *coup d'état* in Czechoslovakia taught us that much. It was also clear that, although the United States would be our shield and chief defence, others in the Western alliance would be expected to play their full part. In Canada, a new nationalism found expression in a new internationalism.

To a country that regards itself as an unmilitary nation, this was a significant change of direction. Few nations like to spend scarce resources on defence. But both St. Laurent and Pearson were committed internationalists. Under their leadership and that of Defence Minister Brooke Claxton the cabinet greatly increased the defence budget. In 1951 a brigade group and air division were formed for Europe, and arms and other equipment provided for allied armies. The rebuilding of the forces cost billions of dollars, absorbed a sizable portion of the budget, and was an impressive commitment — larger in fact than might have been expected of Canada. Support for NATO became the cornerstone of foreign policy in the 1950s, complementing our commitment to the United Nations.

Pearson's involvement in the United Nations (he had been president of the General Assembly at the time of the Korean conflict) convinced him that military preparedness alone was not the best solution. He had serious misgivings when an impetuous US General Douglas MacArthur pushed into North Korea. For Pearson, exclusively military solutions in a nuclear world were just too risky. His whole background had been in conciliation. He saw that as a respected middle power, we might carve out a new role for ourselves as an international negotiator in an enlarged UN.

This approach would soon be put to the test. But this time it would not be a communist aggressor threatening world peace, but the invasion of Egypt by Canada's two motherlands, Britain and France. In 1956, Egypt nationalized the Suez Canal. Outraged at this violation of a treaty only just signed, the British PM, with the help of the French and the Israelis, sent forces to recapture the canal. To most of the world this was gunboat diplomacy at its worst. (The action was all the more deplorable since it took place as Soviet troops repressed an uprising in Hungary. While world attention was diverted, the Russians were able to bring their satellite brutally to heel with hardly a breath of international condemnation.)

The Liberal government had no doubt where its duty lay in the Suez crisis. Pearson saw clearly that the Anglo-French action, which began faltering almost at once, would in the long run be self-defeating and could deal a fatal blow to the Commonwealth, most of whose members were adamantly opposed to such latter-day imperialism. Pearson therefore brought all his negotiating skills to bear to find a face-saving solution whereby the British and French could withdraw.

The formula he eventually steered through the General Assembly called for sending a UN peacekeeping contingent to Egypt to come between the Israeli and Egyptian troops and to allow the Anglo-French force to leave Suez quietly. Pearson's brilliant diplomacy would later bring him the Nobel Prize for Peace.

Canadian participation in that UN peacekeeping operation was but the first such occasion of many, including the Congo (1960), Cyprus (1964), New Guinea (1962), Yemen (1963) and Pakistan (1965). In addition, Canada was part of the tripartite commission set up by the Geneva Conference of 1954 to observe the "peace" in Vietnam, Cambodia and Laos. Indeed, in 1964, our peak year for peacekeeping activity, more than two thousand Canadians were serving that cause around the world. Canada had found a mission in international affairs for which it seemed peculiarly well qualified.

Of course, the peacekeeping role has not been without its drawbacks. It has cost the Canadian taxpayer millions of dollars and has sometimes put a strain on Canada's slender military resources. Since 1964, a brigade has been earmarked for UN service. The improvement of Canada's peacekeeping capabilities was one reason for the unification of the armed forces carried out under Defence Minister Paul Hellyer. (The repercussions of that enforced union are still being felt. At the time it may have seemed a good idea, and perhaps Canada thought the NATO allies would follow our lead. But unification has certainly had an adverse effect on morale).

Peacekeepers, moreover, do not win many friends, since they rarely please either antagonist. And a *sine qua non* of such a role is impartiality — not an easy thing to achieve in a world so starkly divided between communist and non-communist ideologies. When one of Canada's aims has been to enhance the UN influence and encourage peaceful negotiation, it has been particularly galling to be criticized on all sides. Even at home, the government has had to put up with misinformed opposition. This was particularly true during the Suez Crisis, when many Canadians (43 per cent according to one poll taken at the time) were in support of the Anglo-French action. Many Conservatives viewed Liberal support of the UN as a betrayal of our traditional allies and a concession to American pressure.

This was not a new charge. As we have seen, fear of too close ties with the United States has frequently permeated Canadian economic and cultural life, spilling over into foreign relations and continental defence. A stance that will be uniquely Canadian, showing to the rest of the world an independent foreign policy, has been a recurring theme in every Canadian administration, Liberal and Conservative alike. That urge partly inspired Canada's early recognition of mainland China, continuing relations with Castro's Cuba, and a repeated refusal to join the Organization of American States. Any extension of US laws to subsidiaries of American multinational corporations operating in Canada has been vigorously combatted, and Canadian roles in the Commonwealth and in peacekeeping operations have been valued partly because they set Canada apart from the United States. Of course, this stance, too, has its problems, since Canadians are so reliant on US goodwill, especially in the economic sphere. Pearson learned this lesson once again in 1965 when, against advice, he criticized US policies in Vietnam in a speech in Philadelphia. President Lyndon Johnson was not amused; Pearson apologized.

Yet despite periodic differences of opinion and temporary cooling in Canada-US relations, the two countries, knowing that they need one another, have bound themselves together in a continental defence system. In this field, too, Liberal governments have had to tread a delicate path. With the advent of the Soviet Union as a nuclear power, the possibility of an attack on the United States over the Canadian Arctic became a reality. Canada did not have the capabilities nor the technology to defend herself; but neither did we wish to renounce sovereignty over any part of her territory to the United States. Instead, Liberal policy has been to maintain a measure of joint control over the defence system. This is what the North American Air Defence agreement (NORAD) achieved in 1957. Although signed by the new Conservative government, it had been designed during the last years of the previous Liberal one. NORAD, in fact, was the natural outcome of the Liberal approach to managing continental defence in partnership with the United States.

When Pearson became Prime Minister in 1963, there was little doubt that the broad principles of foreign policy would remain the same despite adjustments in how Canada could best contribute to collective security, specifically in NORAD. If NORAD were to be an effective deterrent to Soviet aggression over the North Pole, defence planners contended that nuclear-armed missiles should be placed in Canada. Diefenbaker, in his last sterile year in office, had refused to allow the missiles to be armed. It was a sensitive issue. Many in the Liberal Party, as in the Conservatives and New Democratic, were opposed to having such weapons on Canadian soil.

In 1962, the Soviet Union attempted to place nuclear missiles in Cuba, but in a showdown with the United States, backed off. Many took the threat represented by the Cuban Missile Crisis as a signal for Canada to fulfill its obligations to NORAD. If Ottawa did not now allow NORAD nuclear missiles in Canada, continental defence would be impaired. So with regret but with determination, Pearson, as the Opposition leader, announced that he was convinced that the arming of the missiles should go ahead. The party swung behind him. At the same time, he contended that we should take a hard look at our role in NATO and NORAD to ensure our contribution was both effective and realistic.

Pearson had always shared concerns within NATO itself that not enough emphasis was being put on detente and disarmament, much less on the political, economic and cultural efforts originally seen as

70

an important part of the Atlantic alliance. Such criticisms did not reduce the Liberal commitment to NATO, but did suggest why Pearson, when he formed the government in 1960, reviewed how NATO and Canada's role in it could be improved. Liberal policy under Trudeau broadly followed Pearson's policies. In 1969, Trudeau reaffirmed the continuing Canadian commitment to NATO but announced that the size of our ground and air contribution in Europe would be reduced. The 1971 Defence Forces White Paper identified the protection of Canadian sovereignty as the prime role of our armed forces, with NATO down the list. Several NATO allies feared that Canada was reneging on its treaty obligations, but the reduction was based on a realistic view as to how large Canada's contribution should be. In 1975, however, Trudeau upgraded Canada's commitment as a deterrent to Soviet aggression.

Today the threat of nuclear war is naturally the foreign policy issue of the most fundamental concern to Canadians. As early as 1949, when the Soviet Union became a nuclear power, the St. Laurent government realized that the threat of such a war would henceforth be a fact of life; no amount of wishful thinking, no amount of rhetoric, would make the weapons go away. As a NATO member, Canada supported the deterrent role of nuclear weapons (i.e., the best use of nuclear weapons is never to use them). As a member of NATO and NORAD, Canada could, however, add its influence to the planning of nuclear defence.

At the UN there were disarmament initiatives to be taken, including the control of testing and the non-proliferation of nuclear weapons. Pearson and Trudeau had worked to ensure that NATO — without compromising its strength as a deterrent — would negotiate with the Warsaw Pact to defuse some of the tension. There was some progress, with the Helsinki Agreement signed in 1975. While these negotiations were going on, Canada also weighed in at international conferences to control the spread of nuclear weapons. The United Nations added its voice to the call for arms control. There, in 1978, Trudeau spoke eloquently of the need to control the escalation. He recognized, however, that arms control proceeds only slowly, step by step.

Nuclear proliferation and new delivery systems made more urgent the need to reach mutually acceptable limits on the ability of men to incinerate each other. Clearly the prime responsibility for disarmament remained with the United States and the Soviet Union. Canada's influence may have been less than we would like, but there was no magic by which it could become suddenly more powerful. It was neither in Canada's interest nor in those of global peace and security that NATO's role as a deterrent to war in Europe be undermined. By the late 1970s, the pace of arms control had slowed, with evidence that the Soviet Union had escalated the arms race in an attempt to tip the balance in its own favour. To meet this new Soviet threat, the NATO allies in Europe agreed to deploy the cruise missile. To meet our obligations, Ottawa has signed an umbrella agreement with the United States for weapons testing in Canada, including the unarmed cruise.

Just as successive Liberal governments have been at pains to maintain NATO and NORAD commitments, so too have they fostered links with the Commonwealth. For example, St. Laurent's friendship with Prime Minister Jawaharlal Nehru helped keep India in the Commonwealth once the country gained independence. Canada provided some of the leadership that resulted in the creation of the Colombo Plan, a pioneering programme for subsequent aid to the Third World. And Pearson and Trudeau used all their diplomatic skills to prevent the Rhodesian Crisis from becoming so divisive as to end the Commonwealth.

At the beginning of his days as leader, it was thought that Trudeau might be out of sympathy with the Commonwealth, regarding it as a fading influence in world affairs. But over the years, he came to value its multiracial character and the opportunities and contacts it offers. Indeed, in 1972, the Trudeau government showed courage in accepting large numbers of Asians expelled from East Africa, especially at a time of high unemployment and just before a general election.

Along with support for the Commonwealth has gone an increasing interest in French-speaking countries. In 1970 Canada participated in the initial meetings of the *Agence de cooperation culturelle et techniques des pays francophone,* a loose group composed largely of France's former colonies: in a broad sense a sort of French-speaking Commonwealth. In the past decade, Canada has played an increasingly important part in the countries of *La francophonie,* but for reasons that were partly internal, at least in the beginning. Until the 1960s Canada had little involvement with France's ex-colonies. Although involved in UN peacekeeping operations in the Congo, Canada knew little about most of the other francophone countries of the region. Indeed, until Expo 67 brought representatives of the new African states to Montreal, that part of the world had barely impinged on the Ottawa consciousness. When it did, it was recognized that these countries were turning for help and cultural contacts to Quebec, rather than to Ottawa, with such contacts being actively encouraged by France. This point was made plain in 1968 when Gabon invited Quebec, but not Ottawa, to a francophone conference on education. The Quebec delegation was received with full honours due a sovereign state, with the Quebec flag flying alongside those of the indepedent nations at the conference.

This was too much for Pearson, who had already been offended the previous summer by French President Charles de Gaulle's insolent

Vive le Québec libre speech. He had no intention of letting Gabon get away with such behaviour. When an apology was not forthcoming, he broke off diplomatic relations. Some thought the Liberals were over-reacting but the point had been made. The federal government understood Quebec's natural interest in the countries of French-speaking Africa, but had no intention of letting that interest become a stalking horse for Quebec separatism. Ottawa was in charge of foreign relations. That was the way it was going to stay. Under Trudeau's leadership, tension between Ottawa and Quebec, at least in this area, gradually eased. The *Agence* continues to enjoy the economic and cultural support of both Ottawa and the provincial government of Quebec.

Soon after his election in 1968, Trudeau announced that the Liberal government would undertake a sweeping review of Canada's foreign policy. The time was ripe. As Trudeau put it, "Reassessment has become necessary not because of the inadequacies of the past but because of the changing nature of Canada and the world around us . . . . Canada's position in the world is now very different from that of the postwar years . . . . Now Europe has regained its strength. The Third World has emerged."

His review did not really mark a significant departure from the course the party had pursued since the war. In the 1960s, in addition to our role in the UN and NATO, we became active in building new diplomatic and economic ties outside the Atlantic triangle, with new emerging powers. Ottawa undertook a more rigorous definition of what exactly our national interests abroad were. Yet it was clear that challenges would be met as the old ones had been: by working with other nations within and without the United Nations, NATO, the Commonwealth and *La francophonie.* The Trudeau government was as broadly internationalist as any since the war, but its tone was differ-ent. It saw that Canada could not go on indefinitely being one of the world's helpful fixers, a troubleshooter for peace. Canada's commit-ment to a peacekeeping role would not diminish. But we should be more realistic about what our contribution should be.

One area of foreign affairs that became a particular interest to Trudeau was Canada's relations with the Third World or the so-called North-South dialogue. As an elder statesman of the Common-wealth and an experienced world traveller, Trudeau had the oppor-tunity to see at first hand the grinding poverty, the immense economic and social problems in many newly emerging nations. As far back as 1968, in a speech in Edmonton, he said, "In the long run the over-whelming threat to Canada will not come from foreign investments or foreign ideologies or even — with good fortune — foreign nuclear weapons. It will come instead from the two-thirds of the people of the world who are steadily falling farther and farther behind in their search for a decent standard of living." In recent years, our contacts with the Third World have increased dramatically. Many new envoys have been appointed. The Canadian International Development Agency (CIDA), the International Development Research Centre, and the Canadian University Service Overseas (CUSO), together with official government programmes and non-governmental organizations, have provided a network of aid, advice and technological assistance. This aid is sometimes criticized for being bilateral — that is, committing the recipients to buy goods and services from Canada regardless whether such goods are suitable. Certainly, some Canadian aid is a bit self-serving (though not so much as a decade ago); the Canadian public would be less likely to support such outlays of their taxes if they did not see some return for their cash. Some Canadians have also been wary of the calls for more favourable trading terms for the Third World. The free-trade-versus-protectionist argument, noted earlier, is often conducted as if it were of interest only to the industrialized world. Both the Pearson and Trudeau governments recognized that it was at least of equal interest to developing countries: a further extension of the Liberal commitment to extend compassion and sharing beyond our own borders.

For all the criticism of Canada's aid programme — that it is too much or not enough — the record is one of which Canadians can be justly proud. By 1974 Canadian aid to the Third World had risen to .51 per cent of GNP, a marked improvement from the meagre .19 per cent of 1961. Furthermore, in spite of a few dissenting voices, the Canadian people on the whole support the Liberal government's attitude to sharing our good fortunes. Witness their response to the plight of refugees around the world, particularly the Vietnam "boat people." They are convinced that not only is it in Canada's interests but that it is a moral duty to reach out to the Third World.

That these are times of economic restraint and retrenchment becomes more and more apparent throughout the industrialized world. Recently the United States, that most generous of nations, has channelled more of its resources into military aid to suitably anti-communist nations. In the European Community, protectionism has gained some ground. Even in Britain, the mother country of so many developing nations, prohibitively high fees have closed the universities to students from former colonies. Canada has struggled to achieve an identity distinct from both the colonial past and the Americanized present. One of the many ways we do this is by our compassionate approach to the North-South dialogue.

SAYING ADIEU
TO PIERRE TRUDEAU

I confess it freely: it is difficult to know just how to sum up Pierre Elliott Trudeau. His achievements are obvious enough, indeed conspicuous by their size, importance and number. The history books inevitably will know that it was Trudeau who defused Quebec separatism, made Canada officially bilingual, created the Canadian constitution with its Charter of Rights. But history will be correct only as far as it goes when it fails to pinpoint, as everyone now fails to pinpoint, just how Trudeau changed us so profoundly and fundamentally. All that can be said succinctly at this early date is that he seemed to will change as much through the force of his singular personality as through his actions.

Beyond that I am probably a disappointment to readers expecting fresh insights from a member of the last Trudeau cabinet. It is true that I have known him for some years now, that I was privileged to work with him in caucus and otherwise behind closed doors. But I knew him not at all compared with his oldest and closest friends such as Marc Lalonde, Gerard Pelletier or Jean Marchand who perhaps have known him not all that well either. I trust it will not sound like an evasion to say that it is not in Trudeau's nature to be known but only to be experienced. Perhaps closeness has robbed all of us now living of the necessary perspective. Perhaps historians will have better answers to our questions about Pierre Trudeau. But somehow I doubt it.

In his thoughtful biography *The Northern Magus* (easily, in my view, the best book on Trudeau and the recent era of Canadian politics), Richard Gwyn was forced to conclude that Trudeau's relationship to us was somewhat magical in nature. That is tantamount to saying that it defied understanding. It was a question with which Gwyn as a top Ottawa columnist continued to grapple, and one passage from a recent article of his struck me forcefully. Gwyn was recalling that phenomenon called Trudeaumania by the press in 1968 and how it first wavered, then receded from view. "He let us down and so we turned on him and, in 1972, almost turned him out," wrote Gwyn. "We then re-created him, because he was so stylish and daring and sassy, and as much because he made us proud to have as our roving ambassador a 'priceless asset,' in the phrase of former US vice-president Walter Mondale. From Paris to Peking and from New Delhi to New York, Trudeau sent out the message that not all Canadians were like, well, Canadians."

Which is akin to what Joe Clark must have meant when he called Trudeau "a European Canadian, not a North American Canadian." Some would have said Martian Canadian, reaching for some metaphor to grasp the strangeness which he often exuded and which became, at length, addictive, giving us withdrawal pangs when stopped. Trudeau was unlike, say, Diefenbaker, in that he was a politician wholly suited to governing and wholly unsuited to being in opposition. Yet within a few months of his defeat in the 1980 election, the party had a twenty-point lead in the polls. As much as I should like to ascribe this totally to public recoiling at the infant Clark government, I know that I cannot. Trudeau sometimes infuriated Canadians, but he kept challenging us to be better than perhaps many of us had believed it possible to be. In a strange sort of way, Canada grew up under his tutelage, by turns mocking and intense though it frequently was.

Most of us dimly remember studying paradox as a literary device but are unaccustomed to meeting it in public life. Trudeau, sometimes consciously but most often not, throve on paradox. He was a bitter cynic and a true believer. He was the Jesuit-trained rationalist yet a player of hunches and a slave to instinct. We are accustomed to leaders with carefully controlled public images. We are used to having the politician and the news media locked in a symbiotic — or mutually parasitic — relationship. Trudeau and the media did not particularly take well to each other. He seemed to work around the media as well as through them. What the press and television saw was a figure frequently too complex, in this paradoxical way, to be reported on in the usual manner. Yet however strange he seemed to the general public in his background, personal style and manner of address, Trudeau came to a sympathetic understanding with them almost intuitively, bypassing many of those who would seek to explain the one to the other. In time, I believe, it became apparent to the voters that what they had was what there *was* to be had. No other politician in memory was, in his way, quite so direct, though almost all had been more predictable, more "normal." In comparison with Mackenzie King, for instance, Trudeau laid his personality out on the table for all to see. It is simply that what there was to show in his case was more diverse — more human that is, if certainly not more typical — than what the public had come to expect of a leader.

His offhandedness took getting used to at first. "To be quite frank," he said in announcing his bid for the leadership early in 1968, "if I try to analyze it, well, I think in the subconscious mind of the press it started out like a huge practical joke on the Liberal Party." No less startling was his willingness to deal with unpleasant realities. Of his colleagues in the House he said in 1969: "When they get home, when they get out of Parliament, when they are fifty yards from Parliament Hill, they're no longer honourable members — they're just nobodies." By which he meant that in presentday Canada much of the business of government is inevitably conducted in ministries and departments by civil servants, not in Parliament by MPs: a truth, a sad one perhaps, that is unavoidable, one that always infuriates dwellers in the past of the Diefenbaker stripe. It is also one on which Trudeau seems to have formed his view of the structure of government.

He believed that solely through organization and reorganization of its own procedures could modern government sort out the complex problems it faces. This standpoint was in turn bound up with his belief in the necessity of a strong federal state, one that underlay not only his courageous actions in the October Crisis but his relationship with all the provinces, his persistent drive for the Constitution, his eclectic foreign policy. Many people, mostly Conservatives or Americans, would denounce him as a nationalist, reserving for this epithet their most potent venom. And of course he was a nationalist, but only because he was first a state-ist — hence one who, when looking abroad, saw how interdependent modern states have become. That was one of the ways he fitted snugly into the long crescendo of Liberal theory and history. This and other connections were sometimes obscured by the fact that he was not a party man in the way the term had until then been understood: the back-room boy, the team player, the person who submerges his own personality in the interests of the party. Trying to submerge Trudeau's personality was a sure means of drowning oneself.

He was psychologically incapable of suffering fools gladly if in fact he could suffer them at all. The 1971 exchange which, through the magic of *Hansard* and revisionism, put the word "fuddle-duddle" back into the language, is but the most celebrated instance of many. Most of his utterances were not taken as obscene or even rude but merely as unprimeministerial, as the concept had been understood until his assumption of the spotlight. In London at his last summit conference, only days before the convention to choose a new party leader, Trudeau had implored us President Ronald Reagan to ease the mounting pressure of us-Soviet relations. A flabbergasted Reagan asked, "Pierre, what more can I *do*?" Without missing a beat, Trudeau, never one to mind a little flabbergast, said sharply, "Ron, try harder." Forensically there is no difference between that little exchange and the one in which he ordered the unemployed to pick themselves up, or told the farmers to sell their own wheat instead of looking to Ottawa, or demanded the protesting students grow up. Yet he could be almost anachronistically humble — and genuinely so. In the mid-1970s, release of the so-called Watergate tapes revealed that Richard Nixon had privately referred to Trudeau in the most uncomplimentary terms imaginable relating to the human anatomy. Reporters scurried to Trudeau for his savage riposte. His reply was, "I've been called worse things by worse people."

Previous politicians seemed one-dimensional in comparison. They had made themselves that way to appear as uncomplicated as only people in the press and on television seem. Trudeau was as complex as people in real life. Yet at times he was more theatrical than the most

77

calculating manipulator would have dared be, turning up at a Grey Cup game in a flowing black cape, pirouetting in the presence of the Queen, engaging in shouting matches with hecklers. He cared so much about what he was doing that sometimes he did not give a damn about how it looked. It was of course characteristic of him that he got on more effectively with individuals than with groups, though I believe that Trudeau under full sail was virtually unrivalled as a speechmaker, with his absolutely unique combination of inspiration and charm, and was all but made for television, the route to the largest audiences of all. It was to some extent his talent for more personal communications, his feeling that he could when necessary cut through all the red tape he had helped to create, that led to some dramatic responses. I am thinking of how he reacted to some of the international economic problems that hit Canada particularly hard during his tenure in office.

In 1978, Trudeau, with only one or two advisors, bypassed the whole process of government, the process he loved, admired and understood so well, to intervene directly in slashing government spending. He said later that the plan came to him after he had been out sailing with Helmut Schmidt, the German chancellor. Similarly, in 1982, his initial scheme for keeping down inflation took the form of an amazing one-hour television address which — if one listened between the lines — seemed to tell Canadians to overcome the problem through something like the collective triumph of Nietzschean will. The most striking example, perhaps, is his long peace initiative of 1983-84. It grew out of a career-long, virtually lifelong, devotion to the peace-making process and, significantly, involved personal calls on the many heads of state and world opinion-makers who were the potential combatants. That he was able to approach them again and again as one individual to another speaks well for the esteem in which he was held overseas, an esteem that he did not always attract at home.

Many of the major players in the world political game are those countries which in earlier times had colonial empires, not those like Canada which were the colonized. The Canadian identity crisis may be as hoary and tired a phrase as human lips can form. But what it stands for is undeniably real, in a way almost tangible, and seems to me to derive from the simple fact that we were on the receiving end of the colonizing impulse: from France, especially from Britain and, in the cultural and economic if not the administrative sense, from the United States. This made it difficult for us to see that our position and importance in the world, while fully in keeping with our diverse natural wealth, is also far out of proportion to our population — which is approximately that of Colombia, Yugoslavia or Zaire and only half that, more or less, of Mexico and Vietnam as well as Britain and France. Trudeau by his ease of movement on the world stage made Canadians more aware of our role even as he was expanding it.

Pollsters, analysts, pundits and columnists have never completely fathomed the extent to which this made Canadian voters of all classes go back to the polls again and again and vote for the party of Trudeau. Many may have chuckled in recognition at the infamous crack by David Lewis, pointing to the PM in the House: "There but for the grace of Pierre Elliott Trudeau sits God." But they recognized that, though his weaknesses were always a domestic concern, his strengths were an international matter. As John Gray noted in *The Globe and Mail* on Trudeau's resignation: "The surprising contradiction of the man, of course, is that he was not necessarily without respect among those who did not vote for him, and he was not necessarily liked by those who did vote for him." Canada enjoyed having a man of ideas, a sophisticate, an intellectual who was also a doer, an issuer and a ready accepter of dares, even a master public servant, technician and technologist — all of which he was, superbly. I am biased by temperament and experience in favour of the international viewpoint, but I believe Canadians most liked Trudeau the world statesman, a position he held in addition to that of mere world figure. Millions around the world who remembered nothing else about Canada never forgot that Pierre Trudeau was its Prime Minister. A friend who lived in southern Africa in the early 1970s has told me that there, in remoter villages, people who knew and cared nothing of European politicians knew that Trudeau was leader of the Liberal Party and understood, in a simplified but basically accurate way, what he stood for. This ability to become known round the world was an invaluable aid to Trudeau and Canada in the campaigns for loosening restrictions on world trade, for giving lenient treatment to debt-ridden developing nations, for creating a North-South corridor, for improving the prospects of a lasting East-West peace.

This chapter is brief simply because I do not feel I can say all this any better merely by saying it at greater length. Trudeau did so much in so many different areas that he changed us forever. From this vantage point he would seem to have been the perfect man for the times, and so it is difficult to say to what extent he caused the times to happen as they did and to what extent he was only their willing instrument. When he came to power in 1968, to take one example, the idea of women in cabinet was still fresh and the notion of women in the Supreme Court, and of a woman Speaker of the House or Governor General — all Trudeau accomplishments to come — were practically unthinkable. But all too thinkable was a Quebec forever separated culturally from the rest of Canada and soon perhaps separated politically as well. National unity became his major task to an extent unknown by previous Prime Ministers, even previous Liberal Prime Ministers. A small but highly dramatic, indeed melodramatic, chapter in the long story was the October Crisis. We recall it not only because it showed a level of violence seldom encountered in Canada's official

79

life but because it revealed yet another paradox in Trudeau, normally known as a peace-loving man. A small but vocal percentage of Canadians thought his response too heavy handed, though the over-whelming majority admired the way he stood up to the terrorists and faced them down. No doubt his action made grudging admirers of many who previously had been antagonists and probably would be again. Trudeau could always provoke such alarming shifts in people. His candour and freshness rankled many of the same citizens who ended up admiring him when they observed the natural dignity with which he conducted himself during grave personal upheavals.

He had, depending on one's partisan affiliation, been threatening or promising to resign for quite some time before he actually did so. The first such announcement came in 1979 when he jokingly told the press he wouldn't have them to kick around any more. Then in 1980 he ran to some extent on the promise that, if elected, he would not remain in office long. But he changed his mind later, resolving to stay at least until the Constitution could be duly signed into effect. In 1983 and 1984 he teased newsmen about his future plans or lack of them. In caucus he vowed to us that when he made the decision it would be when the media least expected it. The cat and mouse game was going on only a week before his announcement, on February 29 in leap year 1984, that he would in fact be leaving. He had reached the decision, he said, during a solitary walk through Ottawa's streets in a nocturnal blizzard.

As soon as the news was made public, the Toronto Stock Exchange Composite Index jumped sixteen points and Canadians everywhere suddenly felt sad, whether they admitted it or not.

THE LEADERSHIP

What this little book has tried to show so far is how the Liberal Party has always been the party of consensus, the party that when making policy synthesizes opinion from many quarters, the party that believes the middle ground to be the high ground. As I write these words the party has just chosen John Turner as its new leader, following sixteen years of leadership by Pierre Trudeau. With one era of Liberal politics so obviously at an end and a completely new one so obviously just beginning, it is perhaps understandable that some people might lose sight of this historic principle of consensus and miss the essential continuity of it all. But in fact the leadership convention that took place in June 1984, and the months of spirited campaigning that led up to it, can be taken as the best possible examples of the process so central to an understanding of how the party operates.

Although I was involved in the leadership campaign of John Turner, I was also one of the cabinet ministers kept extra busy in the government by the fact that six of my cabinet colleagues were running. I know well all the men who ran — know some of them quite well indeed — and was naturally privy to certain small incidents and conversations which, cumulatively at least, might add up to a useful insight into what happened. But in recapitulating briefly what took place, my real motivation is more to show how the leadership race revealed the party at its most characteristic and workable.

That many potential candidates for the leadership were considering running long before Trudeau tendered his resignation gradually became evident, thanks in part to the eagerness with which they accepted invitations to even the most remote constituency. But we do not know who among those running decided to go through with it at more or less the last minute. Neither can we know who might have decided earlier but later, before the whistle sounded, decided for various reasons to withdraw. My feeling is that there are those who most felt like running when the party was high in the opinion polls. Conversely, there were others who, imagining themselves capable of some miraculous turn-about feat, felt like running when the party's prospects were dark. These people had several such occasions from which to choose, in 1983 particularly, due to the worldwide recession and the emergence of Brian Mulroney. By the start of the new session of Parliament in December many were jockeying for position, their ears straining for the starting signal.

There seemed to be no question that Turner had been waiting for just such an opportunity ever since he quit the government in 1975. I have always been mystified, however, by the widespread notion that he had somehow, through nine years away from Ottawa, created singlehandedly a political machine to work for him; in fact, he started cold with little in the way of a machine, except for smaller, independent groups formed by others, which he was able to piece together, like a number of small regional railway lines with various gauges of track. It was also apparent that another former Finance Minister — Jean Chrétien, who had the Energy portfolio at the time — would be making up his mind most audibly. He seemed undeterred by the now established tradition dictating that the party shall have anglophone and francophone leaders on an alternating basis. In the end, I believe, this tradition did in fact work against him. His Quebec base was weaker than one might have imagined simply because, when the tradition is maintained, the one-third of the population who are francophones stand to enjoy half the power at least half of the time: a case of a bird in the hand being carefully weighed against two in the bush.

About most of the other candidates who eventually made themselves known there was mostly uninformed speculation. Everyone was naturally awaiting word from the PM. At the new year, the party was judged to be twenty-two points behind the Conservatives in the polls, a stunning decline if true, though not in itself the most important factor. It did seem, however, a special harbinger when combined with the fact that the PM was nearing completion of his personal political agenda, having brought home the Constitution, as promised, having defeated Quebec separatism, as promised, and having steered through many other projects and programmes that were, in his own and the party's view, crucial to the country.

By February there was no secret as to who the other candidates would be but only about who else might join them. All those who later ran were then acknowledged to be making their plans and building up their organizations.

These were a truly diverse lot whose broad range, I believe, illustrates my point about consensus. Justice Minister Mark MacGuigan, representing the left wing of the party, was a protégé of Paul Martin in Windsor, the adopted home they shared; his attraction lay not only in his acknowledged intellectual capacity but in his willingness to confess an insufficiency of charisma. Economic Development Minister Donald Johnston, a humane man and a former tax lawyer, came to the race with respect in the business community, particularly in Quebec, and would eventually emerge a more fully rounded figure in the public mind. John Munro, of Hamilton, the Minister of Indian Affairs and Northern Development who had virtually made that portfolio his personal property through his natural affinity for it, was a scrapper and a fighter. Another leadership candidate from cabinet was John Roberts. Then there was Eugene Whelan, the perpetual Minister of Agriculture, also an Ontarian and (this is not commonly remembered) the oldest veteran of cabinet to run, indeed its most experienced politican, having entered municipal politics in south-western

Ontario when he was twenty-one and having remained in one elected position or another for almost forty years. At the time of which I write, however, it seemed likely — certainly there was much private and public speculation — that others would consider running, especially Jim Coutts, the Prime Minister's former principal secretary who had been narrowly defeated in a by-election in 1981, and Paul Hellyer, who already enjoyed the unique distinction of having run for the leadership of both major parties (the Liberals in 1968, the Tories in 1979), to say nothing of having founded a party of his own. Other names bandied about included those of three women: Judy Erola and Monique Begin from cabinet and Iona Campagnola, the party president. They came at a time when there certainly needed to be serious women candidates for this and most lesser posts. But, alas, all three in the end declined to run. I suspect that in the case of some of these women, as in the case of many heirs apparent and presumptive, the reason they did not materialize as contenders was that the consensus process had already begun.

As organizations are built up, there is inevitably much coining of favours and redemption of old ones. Some look upon this back-room aspect as the darker side of politics, but having seen it at close range I can tell you that it can sometimes be the most noble, if not exactly the most obviously so. It is at that stage that people swap their support and endorsements and other almost tangible assets in order to ensure the integrity, in someone else's platform, of those ideas that they believe it most important for the party to maintain. It is in this manner that positions became planks in the party's platform and that the chemical process of consensus-making begins to boil and bubble. Jim Coutts and Paul Hellyer might fairly be said to stand like bookends at the leftwing and the rightwing of the party, respectively. In deciding not to run, they may have given certain of their beliefs new life and influence in the form of other people who needed their explicit or (more probably) their tacit support. This was one of the first stages in the process of moving both ends towards the sane and sensible centre — not always the same centre as last time, but the workable average of many unworkable extremes, the position best suited to present realities.

For a number of reasons it is perhaps instructive to compare the leadership with the contest for the Democratic presidential nomination that took place in the US concurrently. The comparison is of course cumbersome because compared with our own, the American leadership race is such an extended torture, with the litany of state caucuses and primaries, leading to the general election in which one votes for the person and not the party, which is to say for the image and not the substance. But all that aside, it did indeed seem plain that Walter Mondale, the presumed victor, would not be handed the nomination on a platter but would have to fight every inch of the way despite a substantial advantage in delegate support virtually from the beginning. Such was the situation in the Liberal Party, too. It was announced in the beginning that Turner would not simply be invested with the leadership but would have to battle it out. And then, too, just as the American situation showed some broad interest in the presence or absence of ideas (Mondale finally got the edge on Gary Hart by showing Hart's promises of fresh ideas to be hollow), so there was a similar concern with policy differences across the wide spectrum of candidates here. Yet the spark and crackle of debate also revealed essential similarities as much as it exposed sometimes gaping and sometimes subtle differences.

On March 24 the six candidates who had declared thus far (at that time it still appeared others might enter) debated together for the first time, before two thousand delegates to a Liberal meeting in Toronto. It became clear immediately that women and youth would be major beneficiaries in the ensuing race, regardless of its outcome. Specific issues raised included ways of ensuring that private industry give equal work for equal pay. This was in addition to the whole question of youth unemployment, with proposals ranging from more incentives for private industry to a revised unemployment insurance scheme designed to pay for job creation. Generally speaking, it was obvious that the party was as at least as much interested in economic issues as in social ones and that in the former category was moving a bit to the right. This was underscored for me when MacGuigan, in a tip of the hat to one of Trudeau's Bartlett-quality quotations, said, "We have to get government out of the boardrooms of the nation." He, Munro and Roberts, incidentally, were as one in thinking that Ontario should become bilingual as quickly as possible as a means of reassuring Quebec, as much as a convenience to its own citizenry. This brought to the surface the unease many felt about remarks made some time earlier by Turner, remarks which had threatened to damage him before the race was really begun.

When announcing his bid for the leadership, Turner had let it be known, or at least strongly implied, that he considered French-language rights in Manitoba a provincial, not a federal issue, in the first instance. He thus seemed to run counter not only to the recent policy of the Liberals but indeed the policies of the Tories and the New Democrats and everyone else save possibly the Libertarians. This was no slip of the tongue, however. It was a case of Turner demonstrating right at the outset that he held strong views which cried out for agreement or disagreement. He was holding out the possibility of suasion, not on that point alone, but on policy in general. Such at least is my view: that this promised well for the democratic nature of the entire exercise we were beginning to witness.

No surprise at all, except perhaps in its intensity, was the strength Jean Chrétien displayed from the outset. He has long enjoyed popularity both in party circles and with the generality of his fellow Canadians. His considerable native shrewdness has been proved again and again. Take, for instance, the way he rose to the occasion of being Finance Minister without the formal or practical economic training usually expected of those in that senior position. His popularity extends to the West where it is so crucial the party regain some of its former strength. It rests, I believe, on his ties to the party's historical momentum as well as on his own highly personal style, one not unlike the populist appeal of Diefenbaker in 1958. (Jean will hoot me down for comparing him, even favourably, with the Conservative Diefenbaker, but the comparison is a valid one that flatters them both.)

Chrétien is a wonderfully instinctual politician, who knew when and how to deliver the type of inspirational barn-burner of a speech for which he is justly renowned, when to disregard the advice of his more cautious senior advisors to put more visible distance between himself and Trudeau. For Chrétien had no need to strike a revisionist pose. Problems unknown in earlier years called for new responses. These alone were, he appeared to think, sufficient to distinguish him from the camp of the outgoing leader. Chrétien was actually eager to let people see his links with the past, not just with the Trudeau years but historically and almost genetically with the broad sweep of the party. His father had met Laurier. That sort of hand-that-shook-the-hand idea seemed very fitting.

All of which is to suggest that, even in its early stages, the leadership race had no assured outcome but was, as the pundits kept saying, a horserace. There was of course no surprise in the fact that, in the first furlong or so, Turner, near the rail, seemed to be leading by several lengths, with Chrétien gaining more than the handicappers had anticipated. But the question, to continue with this pari-mutuel metaphor just a moment longer, was not only who would win and who would place but also who would show. The spirited action in the field was especially interesting because it demonstrated the weaving in and out of small political realities and the larger issues, the practical and the theoretical. The combustion generated by this race-within-a-race would inevitably exert pressure on the first- and second-place candidates and hence on policy.

First one must address the question of why there were so many people running. In the middle of the leadership campaign, the *Toronto Star* required nearly an entire page to suggest that megalomania was the only answer. The newspaper polled various psychologists who compared the extent of one candidate's apparently egomaniacal delusions with those of the others. I agree that lack of ego has seldom prevented anyone from running who might otherwise have wished to. But the candidates for this leadership each had some opportunity to emerge the winner or to be of importance in selecting him.

In 1961, John Robarts came in third on the first ballot during the Ontario Conservative leadership convention and quickly emerged the victor as the result of a deadlock. Then, in 1979 Joe Clark narrowly became federal Conservative leader on the fourth ballot after running third behind Brian Mulroney and Claude Wagner on previous rounds. That provided a vivid example and strong incentive for potential power brokers, notwithstanding the fact that Clark proved so riotously unable to hold onto the job once he got it. In Liberal terms, this scenario was even more useful than precedents in other parties would suggest. In a party that governs by compromise when it seems truly the best way for the majority — in a party that can be said to have institutionalized compromise — the thought of ascending to the leadership as a compromise candidate has added allure. But of course the more important consideration, though not the most obvious one, was that of influencing the party's future direction.

It seemed apparent to virtually everyone that this leadership convention was more important than past ones had been. The Trudeau epoch was concluding at a time when, putting momentary ups and downs aside for the moment, the very basis of liberalism, small-l, was under vicious attack on all fronts. By their presence, contenders were imploring the party to retain certain beliefs in the restructuring to follow or to adopt others from among the many available. There were painful choices ahead. By fighting the fight as best he could, a candidate, even one with a relatively narrow base of support among the convention delegates, could attract attention to his views as almost never before.

What might have been the altruistic motives of John Munro, for example? Munro was one of the most effective Indian Affairs ministers we have ever had as I believe any survey of native people would confirm; he also had support of almost legendary solidity from his constituency in Hamilton, to whose hard-working blue collar families he spoke with easy familiarity. But of course that hardly made him an important national draw. During the campaign one sometimes heard it put about that he was in the race as a stalking horse for Chrétien, as a spoiler for Turner, but that was nonsense. He was in the race because of his conviction that, with the federal New Democrats sinking ever lower in national esteem, the Liberals should move not rightwards but leftwards where they belonged — and incidentally scoop up that support itself. If only by providing a contrast, then, Munro, I think, helped underscore what is more and more the single most interesting phenomenon of the campaign and of the present political era: the rise of what is sometimes called neo-liberalism, a term I dislike but whose usefulness I recognize.

The word refers to a pragmatic sort of liberalism which in the future can only grow. It is one that can be characterized, I suppose, by a devotion to economic issues, not at the expense of social ones, but before them. Other touchstones range from an optimistic belief in better power-sharing between and among the regions (as distinct therefore from the increased centralization espoused by Munro) to

86

something as specific as programmes to encourage research into high technology. It was no accident that most of the likely candidates for that third spot eventually won by Donald Johnston could easily be identified with some or most of the neo-liberal ideas. There is even a case to be made for the statement that they went up in popularity in direct proportion to how totally they subscribed to these views. Johnston, for example, was one of the most vocal in his desire to slash the deficit, leave job creation to the private sector, and so on. That is on the one hand. On the other hand, he garnered enormous respect for something that would have cost the career of a US political candidate: for breaking down, the voice aquiver and eyes misty, during a speech, so strongly did he feel the truth of what he was saying. It was a speech about the absolute necessity of disarmament talks between the US and the Soviets. That mixture of right and left, in those proportions, is the heart of the country's present mood. In this respect, the convention was a more accurate reflection of the temper of the times than the media seemed to be — the media which have been uncharacteristically slow to define and popularize the new liberal spirit. That is to suggest that the delegates were, it was heartening to see, more interested in the issues oftentimes than in the personalities. Or at least the show biz considerations so beloved by the public were not a significant factor in the race for third place, where instant public recognition was not a crucial factor. For instance, Donald Johnston, even compared to the others little known and (I say this with affection) undramatic, was the third-choice leader from early on and seemed to get stronger as the contest lengthened. The reason: he was in tune with the party's mood, with the spirit of the majority of its thinkers. He emphasized such hard economic realities as lower capital gains taxes to bolster investment and more help in science and technology (particularly in research and development). The lesson: this was serious business. In fact, it was gratifying to see just how seriously he took the issues and how seriously the convention took him.

As the leadership process reached into May, with about six weeks remaining to the convention at the Ottawa Civic Centre, it was clear that the combat between Turner and Chrétien would be bloody. Chrétien began to imply that Turner had deserted the party and the country by quitting the Trudeau cabinet, and as time went on he tended to accuse Turner by name. Also, each man took the other to task for having, where his policies should exist, a big vacuum which, like nature, each fellow claimed to abhor. For two people supposedly devoid of plans or policy, they both marshalled a considerable array of precise information on what they would undertake, and in doing so pointed up substantial differences. Turner, for example, consistently spoke to the urgency of cutting the deficit whereas Chrétien, though concerned, thought the matter bound to external circumstances and could perhaps be lived with at present levels a while longer: no trifling difference. On other issues, however, there was a general mutuality of preference, showing the core feeling of the party and making clear that paper differences were not being created for the sake of the campaign. In one memorable instance — on the question of whether to increase foreign aid — even Brian Mulroney, without being asked, remarked that, yes, he too would increase it, thereby getting a mention in the press on a day when the country's attention was elsewhere. Generally, though, democracy was at its strongest when Turner and Chrétien espoused strongly held opposing views. Each man's ideas grew out of his own social, economic and political milieu. Turner (whom Peter C. Newman once called "the Honourable Member from Winston's" a reference to a favourite luncheon spot of Bay Street financiers) said he believed that "sectoral" free trade with the US, particularly in agriculture, was worth a try. Chrétien was less sure and less prepared to experiment. I like to imagine (it is the romantic and the historian in me coming out) that this is because he has ancestral memories, unsuitable to articulation but very strong, of what the free trade issue did to Laurier in 1911 — destroyed him.

At the ides of May, matters were very close indeed. In those sections of the country where one man or the other enjoyed a large natural allegiance, the results were surprising. Turner seemed to be ahead in Ontario over all, but there had been one rather surprising attempt against him in Metro Toronto. Chrétien was naturally strong in Quebec but the outcome there was a bit of a seesaw. The Maritimes seemed to favour Turner by a narrow margin. Of delegates committed in the West, Turner held the support of a plurality of those in Manitoba and Saskatchewan with Chrétien having equivalent strength in Alberta and BC (John Munro, it should be noted, held sway in the Far North, his one area of strength outside the Hamilton region.) Of 3,534 delegates to the convention, still at this point about a month away, fully 1,000 were from the West, fully forty per cent were women, though with less strength than that would suggest. About 700 of the delegates were Young Liberals, most of whom had literally grown up with Trudeau as leader. Turner claimed by the end of the month to have strength enough to get the leadership on the first ballot. Chrétien claimed he had enough support to prevent him from doing so.

The longer the race went on, the more assured and poised Turner became, a change noted by the delegates and by the press or most of it. (I was amused to see some reporters ascribe sinister motives to Turner's change in fashion, from dark suits in the first part of the campaign to something slightly more sporty a little later on. But according to Richard Gwyn, this had nothing to do with the advice of highly paid image consultants bent on manipulating people's minds. It stemmed from the fact that the Turner household had suffered an infestation of moths in an upstairs closet. This revelation worried me since the Turners and MacLarens are next door neighbours.)

Anyway, the polls and still more polls confirmed the increasing momentum of Turner, though victory was by no means assured, much less a quick one. Increasingly, though, it seemed clear that Turner was not only the man best able to lead the party victoriously against the Conservatives, by now in their strongest position in a generation, but the best able to accommodate the concerns of the main Liberal factions and mould them into a cohesive and workable engine of the voters' will. For there was danger that the elemental differences between the traditional liberals and the neo's — characterized by the economic interventionism of Chrétien, MacGuigan, Roberts, Whelan and Munro on the one side and the deficit-cutting stance of Turner and Johnston on the other — could become wounds in need of treatment. Turner seemed to me not only the best choice for leader but the best available physician should one be called for.

Ten days before the end of the campaign, Turner reduced his level of activity, going from five public appearances per day to only one, and travelling less accordingly. All told he had personally talked to, by his own estimate, 2,500 of the delegates. With days to go before the convention, Richard Doyle, the editor emeritus of the *Globe and Mail,* wrote this: "It requires a veritable cornucopia of hypotheticals to put together a scenario in which John Turner could lose the convention which will choose the next prime minsiter of Canada."

At the eleventh hour, both the Turner and Chrétien camps released new polls seeming to prove quite contradictory claims. But it was the Turner poll, indicating that a party led by him would have the best chance of defeating a Conservative party led by Brian Mulroney, that rang the truest and stuck in people's minds. For it was this consideration, in the end, that it all came down to. Here at its bluntest and most obvious perhaps was the Liberal pragmatism I have been speaking of. The story of the convention that began Friday, June 14, 1984, was the story of how the other factions would induce Turner to accommodate their own views in return for greater support of him. In other words, the same pragmatism, the same unalterable drift towards the acceptable and workable middle ground, but in a vastly complicated, far more subtle way. This is what I found made the convention so exciting. Under the ceiling of balloons, beneath the high curtain of noise, behind the smoke and claustrophobic motion of eleven thousand people jammed into the Civic Centre, there was the audible and unmistakable rhythm of emerging consensus. It was a beat that would have been instantly recognizable to Laurier or King.

Perhaps because the party had not witnessed a leadership convention in almost a generation, there was a great deal of long-pent-up enthusiasm but no sense on anyone's part of having forgotten how to do it or how to behave. The field was less overcrowded this time (in

1968 there had been nine candidates). For this and many other reasons the energy was more concentrated, if also less evenly, with the two frontrunners as the foci. When the candidates spoke on the opening evening, it was the last occasion to display their wares. It was their last opportunity to influence delegates directly on the basis of the positions they had taken. It was the final confirmation of who had risen in the standings and by how much. Most candidates had certainly gained by their efforts, but most eyes were on Turner and Chrétien, both of whose speeches were good illustrations of how the party keeps moving towards its own centre as it goes. Listening to each man showed how the consensus mechanism brings everything into focus.

Often criticised (or cheered, depending on the critic) for his patriotic, emotional, off-the-cuff and, I find, always effective speeches, Chrétien was drawn by the great invisible magnet into a prepared text touching on such weighty yet down-to-earth matters as Canada's role in the world. He placed himself in the position of something like a statesman and gave a marvellous speech. Turner, for his part, usually speaks in a staccato fashion from three-by-five cards, but that night was wonderfully fluent and continuous and highly charged; he spoke in a style that reinforced the substance. Ultimately, though, speeches are little more than signs, barometric readings, not events in themselves. Turner's showed that the strength of some of his opponents, who stood to his political left, had drawn to the surface his own more moderate instincts. Thus, the speech confirmed the need for a net of social services and similar parts of the liberal philosophy. Each man made his most important speech to date and it was probably each man's best, if not most representative.

The crunch, of course, came Saturday, June 16, the day of the voting, with a great deal of disagreement about what in fact the first ballot count would be. For a few hours the Civic Centre probably became North America's largest gambling den.

The tedious and nerve-wracking voting process began at about two o'clock. Before it had been underway long, External Affairs Minister Allan MacEachen threw his support to Turner. Then came signs that Munro was losing most of his northern and native delegates to Turner — even though Chrétien himself had been immensely popular as Minister of Indian Affairs and Northern Development. One of the most vocal displays came later in the afternoon when the mayor of Edmonton (a key MacGuigan supporter) went over to Turner, prefiguring the end for MacGuigan. Shortly after five p.m. the results of the first ballot were made known:

Turner	1,593	MacGuigan	135
Chrétien	1,067	Munro	93
Johnston	278	Whelan	84.
Roberts	185		

As the bottom man, Whelan was eliminated, and he gave such support as he had to Chrétien. Moments later MacGuigan strode into Turner's camp. The whole process was nakedly apparent now.

Turner was one hundred and twenty-five votes shy of the simple majority he needed. Munro then went over to Chrétien, but found few of his supporters going with him. Roberts, too, moved towards the populism of Chrétien. Much attention now focused on Johnston but he refused to give in to entreties by the Chrétien people or for that matter the Turner people. The results of the second ballot were read at eight-thirty that evening: Turner 1,862 . . . Chrétien 1,368 . . . Johnston 192. Something like human fireworks filled the enormous hall.

So John Turner was to be Canada's seventeenth Prime Minister. Almost at once he began an acceptance speech aimed both at healing whatever wounds had resulted from the selection process and at the preparing for the general election which could not now be far distant. Looking very much in charge and very much the leader, he was met with wild enthusiasm. It was an exuberant moment when all seven contenders lined up on stage to be joined by Pierre Trudeau. For a moment, the historic past, the recent past and the present dissolved into a single future.

LIBERAL THOUGHTS
ON CANADA'S FUTURE

Even as the janitors swept away the debris of three days of convention, delegates knew that the Canada beyond the walls of the Ottawa coliseum would present the next government with formidable economic and social challenges. There was some reassurance in statistics that recovery did seem to be underway, but the recent recession had been deep and its effects pervasive. There would be a long hard haul ahead.

The world recession had hit Canada when we had barely finished congratulating ourselves on successfully if tardily acquiring a constitution. Despite the warnings of such jeremiahs as the Bank of Canada, most of us were unprepared for such a rapid decline in economic expectations, especially in view of what the long-term pattern had been.

Since 1945 or so and along with the other industrialized and even some developing countries, Canada had enjoyed unparalleled economic growth. Canadians began to acquire what they began to desire: large, baroque automobiles, more elaborate housing and the myriad of electrical and mechanical gadgets that had so captured the imagination of those rapidly emerging from wartime austerity. The u-drive helicopters, a favourite product of hyperimaginative postwar artists, did not materialize, but almost everything else was delivered more or less on schedule.

Even after making every possible allowance for inflation, the fact remains that our standard of living grew at a remarkable rate throughout those consistently optmistic postwar decades. In both Western Europe and North America, governments, frequently led by liberals or social democrats, complacently presided over economic growth, full employment, and greater equality of opportunity. Redistributed income and enhanced social programmes all combined to protect the environment, support higher education, improve working conditions and open at least some new opportunities for working women. Further progress was confidently predicted on the West's continuing industrial ascendancy. It was also assumed that public investment would play a greater role, that national planning of one sort or another would emerge, and that international trade would expand. Deficit financing would reduce or eliminate what were seen as transient problems in an inexorable trend upwards.

During this time, we Canadians received far more than we had ever dreamt of — and our country changed almost beyond recognition. There was a massive influx of largely European immigrants, eager to join in the unwonted prosperity and to escape the immediacy of a cold war. Combined with a temporarily high birth rate, this meant that the population grew rapidly, even if it remained miniscule in global accounting. Equally important, we had become yet more urban, decidedly less parochial, better educated, and consequently more complex in our attitudes and continuing expectations. Values evolved, beliefs changed, a sexual revolution and a new world of instantaneous communication challenged stodgy Canadian thinking. Even the conviction that government spending could somehow solve most if not all of society's problems, including even federal-provincial differences, had taken a firm grip on the Canadian imagination. This understandable assumption, however, masked more fundamental questions which, for a time at least, Canadians could avoid. To what degree should decentralization in an increasingly industrialized trading nation proceed? A few of us began to ask ourselves whether there was some point at which being a nation began to lose its meaning. Did collective action for our mutual benefit have some limits? Heresy of heresies, some began to ask whether the postwar "welfare state" was really a success. We slowly recognized that, to a disturbing degree, many Canadians were still denied dignity, decency and opportunity, especially the aged, female heads of families and the "working poor" (those employed but receiving inadequate incomes). Of course the definition of poverty had evolved — the possession of a television set had become a *sine qua non* of Canadian citizenship — but some of us began to ask whether much progress had been made, for example, in ensuring that pensions, both public and private, were adequate.

Our social development was based on the assumption of steady economic growth. That growth was, in turn, based on cheap energy and increasing international demand for our apparently abundant raw materials. The happy expectation that our standard of living would always increase contributed to the tacit assumption that we were somehow entitled to an array of expensive social services — education, pensions, medicare, unemployment insurance — which could always be financed from our steadily increasing prosperity.

Gradually, however, a few clouds, no bigger than your fist, appeared. Somehow it seemed that cheap energy and international demand for our raw materials could no longer be taken for granted in quite the same way. Other countries, with higher rates of productivity, were beginning to produce many of the very same goods upon which western prosperity, Canada's included, had traditionally been based. Unfamiliar faces were starting to appear among those who supply the world with its sophisticated manufactured goods. The idea of a Japanese automobile had once been absurd; now there were Japanese automobiles on Canadian streets — and they were better than Canadian or American ones. For more than a century, national resources had been the sure underpinning of our economic growth. By the 1970s, however, it began to be recognized that other countries could,

94

for example, produce that all-Canadian product, nickel, more cheaply than Sudbury could, thereby winning for themselves an increasing share of a world market that would, in any case, be smaller as new materials replaced old. And what was the future of copper when a satellite could do the job of a thousand miles of wire? Pulp and paper had long been as Canadian as maple syrup, but now the southern United States and even some developing countries could, in fifteen years or so, grow trees suitable for certain paper production. What did that mean for Canada where fifty years or more was required and where, in any event, we had not only extravagantly cut but parsimoniously replanted? What was more, other countries, through higher rates of saving, were denying themselves present consumption in favour of future consumption. The pervasive nature of new technology was impelling the world towards greater interdependence, rendering various international institutions, born in postwar hopes of selfless co-operation, decidedly less able to cope with new demands.

But even as the familiar trading world was being altered by dynamic and insistent new players, inflation called into question the whole international economic order. In the face of simultaneous inflation and economic stagnation, the public mood of the western democracies changed from optimism to growing misgiving. During the postwar period, big government had been welcomed as the means of overcoming inequality of opportunity. When, to everyone's surprise, it became apparent that the pie was no longer growing, public opinion shifted from willing acceptance of greater spending and intervention to growing scepticism and frustration. Instead of tolerating big government, many began to see it as an obstacle to economic growth. Over-taxed and over-governed citizens, although still quick to seek specific programmes of interest to themselves, nevertheless became convinced that government had somehow become part of the problem, not part of the solution. As early as 1949, Pearson, swimming against the tide, had sensed the implications of governments taking more responsibility for the direction and even the control of the economy. He wrote: "Whether it desires it or not, that role is being forced on the state by insistent and increasing demands for services and assistance, many of which are made by those who subseqently complain of the interference by government in their affairs . . . . It is, in fact, becoming increasingly difficult to reconcile the satisfaction of such demands with the maintenance of that spirit of self-reliance and competitive achievement which is one of the foundations of our free society." By the 1970s, certain institutions originally intended to help improve society, had become bastions for special interest groups. Already inflation was taking hold to such an extent that the unthinkable, un-Keynesian phenomenon of concurrent inflation and unemployment began to emerge world wide. In the midst of such rapid change, some Canadians looked to the future with misgivings, concerned only to preserve their comforts and what they believed to be eternal verities. Others, however, recognized that the social reform agenda remains long. I am thinking, of course, of the Liberal Party and the governments it has formed. There is still much to do, to say the least.

The pensions of many, for example, are inadequate and their portability limited. The position of the elderly, an increasing proportion of the Canadian population, makes pension improvement, both public and private, an urgent priority. Despite the fact that women now form almost one-half of paid labour and perform most of the unpaid work in the home, many women still end their lives in poverty. In fact, three out of four women today over sixty-five who reside alone live in a bleak existence below the poverty level. The reason is simple: less than one-third of female workers are covered by private pension plans and one-half of all male private pension plans have no survivor benefits. To ensure that this does not continue, pensions must be designed to match more closely the needs of the aged. Also, we must find some way to include homemakers in the Canada Pension Plan. There can be no erosion of medicare, either, for that would hit hardest at those who can least afford it.

Much of our family support system has been in place for forty years. The changing nature of the family — and for better or for worse, it is changing — means a growing number of single-parent families with their own particular needs. It is time to review family allowances, spousal exemption, child tax credits, etc., to make certain that the poorest Canadians, especially those with small children, are receiving the largest share of assistance. What, for example, is the justification for continuing the income tax exemption for dependent children when it benefits the affluent but not the poor who pay no income tax? And why do we delay modifying the present social security system so that it no longer discourages full or part-time employment, thereby penalizing the working poor? When will we speed up our process of helping the handicapped pursue more gratifying lives?

Women are still largely concentrated in less rewarding, less innovative jobs and some of those jobs will be eliminated by microtechnology. Planning and re-training, as well as protective health measures, are all vital. By the turn of the century, women will probably participate in the work force almost in the same numbers as men. Although the average woman spends more time in school than the average man, she earns today about sixty cents for every dollar a man earns. To eliminate these anachronistic discrepancies, we need now more vigorous affirmative action, both public and private.

Among aboriginal Canadians, poverty, illness, and limited educational opportunities are still terrible problems. In fact, native peoples and other visible minorities, as well as recent immigrants who do not conform to the long dominant culture, face many obstacles in their daily lives. Canadians have come a long way from the outright racism of our earlier years; the discrimination, for example, that could bar all Chinese immigrants from citizenship merely on the basis of ethnic origin. But there is still some way to go. The new Charter of Rights will certainly help, and tests in the courts will tell how good a safeguard it is. No charter, however, can legislate people's attitudes; these, too, must change as a result of persuasion and example.

Even more fundamentally, progress in social reform will depend on our economic growth, especially the reduction in our current high levels of unemployment. With a jobless rate of over ten per cent, government revenue declines and social costs soar. A further challenge arises from the fact that, unlike during previous recessions, much unemployment today is what economists call structural unemployment. That is to say that even as our economic growth picks up and additional employment is created, there will not be the same kind of jobs as before. Old industries — steel, automobiles, coal and textiles — industries that were the motor of the industrial expansion of the nineteenth and twentieth centuries — are becoming so-called sunset industries. In Ontario, for example, one in six jobs currently depends on the automobile industry. Even the most optimistic estimates concede an employment decline in the future. In order for us to remain competitive with imported cars, perhaps as many as one-third of the jobs in the Canadian auto industry will be lost. Yet, new industries, the sunrise industries in the service field, in electronics and in biochemistry, to name a few, offer fresh opportunities. Training and re-training will help some displaced Canadians find employment in a rapidly changing industrial world, but how much adaptability can be expected from a steel worker with thirty years' seniority? Dislocation will be inevitable and Liberal policies must ease the transition for everyone caught by this and similar change. Innovative ideas such as work-sharing and a shorter work week will help, along with a more imaginative use of unemployment insurance, but as we shall see, the real solution to these difficult transitional problems will come only through more co-operation among business, government and labour.

That both unemployment and job dislocation are now global problems is no source of comfort. Canadians have come to realize that we must move into new technological fields, but in that recognition we are hardly alone or among the first. International competition will be keen. There are already specific areas in which it is impossible to catch up with such global giants as Japanese electronics firms. That is all the more reason why we need to be clearer about our industrial opportunities.

Unfortunately, "industrial strategy" has become one of those universal and rather tiresome phrases tossed about with little or no clear understanding. It is a great favourite of the NDP in particular, to

97

whom it seems to mean pouring more and more public money into vain efforts to retain jobs in dying industries. What is needed instead, of course, are various forms of government encouragement — tax incentives, help in finding foreign markets, etc. And these must be geared to areas where Canada is developing special expertise. For all its support of megaprojects in the post-C.D. Howe years, the party understands that such projects may be too capital-intensive in the future. It is important to hold in mind that most jobs in Canada are in businesses with fewer than fifty employees and that most of the innovative ideas are initiated by smaller firms. But though small business has increasingly become a major source of our future economic growth, fully ninety per cent of research and development money still goes to the larger firms and government-owned corporations. From now on we shall have to pay greater attention to small teams of adventurous young people with innovative ideas; they are often on the cutting edge of scientific advance.

Also high on the agenda will be the need to expand and diversify further our exports. We have noted how illiberalism flourishes during recession. At home, one's willingness to share is eroded by uncertainty about the future; labour and business become more antagonistic towards each other, the provincial and the federal governments more at loggerheads than usual. In our relations with other countries, this same illiberalism manifests itself in protectionism. As jobs go down, trade barriers go up. And recession emboldens those who, in either good times or bad, are unwilling to assist developing countries. Liberals, traditionally free traders, will want to spurn the siren call of protectionism whose baleful notes have recently been heard througout the industrialized world. With more automobiles, television sets and computers arriving from developing countries at the same time that economic recession has spread across the globe, an increasingly complex web of non-tariff barriers, partl to protect local jobs, has been rapidly woven by industrialized countries. By the late 1970s, the whole magnificent postwar achievement embodied in the GATT began to look a little thin. Agriculture everywhere, including Canada, is hedged about with protectionist devices, and such industries as steel, shipbuilding and textiles are propped up with subsidies and cartels. The automotive and machine tool industries began to look on such arrangements with increasing envy. But these and other excesses promise a future that does not work.

One in three jobs in Canada depends directly or indirectly upon our exports, but the trade barriers of other countries can eliminate those jobs. The calamitous and pervasive impact of protectionism is not limited to hapless workers. Consumers everywhere pay more if they cannot purchase from the cheapest supplier. International bankers do not recover their loans if the borrower is unable by his exports to earn the cash needed for repayment. Raw or semi-

98

processed materials protected at home may mean that a foreign competitor can manufacture his products more cheaply than can Canadians.

Liberal arguments for supporting global free trade are many, various and not always readily understood. Protectionism, by contrast, is simple. Jobs are seen to be on the line and lost jobs are highly visible. Only governments can tally up the total national benefit and decide, in everyone's interest, not to succumb to the wiles of the protectionists. This is not an easy task at any time, especially during a recession. It must include more consultation with labour, an area in which the party must do better.

While Liberals will continue to press for global free trade, the benefits of free trade with the United States alone are less evident. Since the Reciprocity Treaty of 1854, the merits of free trade with the United States have been canvassed extensively (notably in the election of 1911 but also, less publicly, in cabinet discussions of the late 1940s). Indeed, the debate, along with other such perennials as a causeway to Prince Edward Island, has gradually taken on a comfortable familiarity. Arguments on both sides, by both Liberals and Conservatives, have become largely predictable. There is, however, nothing surprising in the durability of this continuing debate. Each generation must ask itself anew how Canada and the United States can best share a continent. Today that assessment will need to take into account current uncertainties facing the manufacturing industry in the two countries and the massive and unprecedented growth in Canada's manufactured imports. Economic relations between Canada and the United States have assumed a more complex character and that complexity will increase. At the conclusion of the GATT Tokyo Round in 1979, Canada committed itself to virtual free trade with the United States in manufactured products by 1988. By then ninety-six per cent of Canadian exports to the US will cross the border tariff free or encounter only a nuisance tariff of five per cent or less.

This, it might be thought, would bring joy to the advocates of US-Canada free trade. But even the faithful are not so naive as to believe that what appears to be free trade would in fact be free trade. Enterprising Canadian companies would no longer encounter many tariffs in attempting to sell into the US market, but they would certainly continue to encounter other barriers, including ones erected by the various state governments. Without greater mutual understanding, non-tariff barriers will continue to plague both Canadians and Americans long after the final tariff has been forgotten. Unless great care were taken, bilateral free trade, or indeed even freer trade, could favour yet more plant concentration in the United States.

In the face of these and other adverse factors, some devotees of free trade offer an alternative: a continuing negotiation to allocate the supposed benefits of free trade between the two countries. The notion might be feasible if the two states were more or less equal in economic and political clout (the European Community provides no model, since the several weaker members have some opportunity, in various combinations, to advance their interests). In a commission of only two countries, the one with greater power would be tempted to use it to satisfy various domestic demands. Furthermore, Canadian sovereignty — the opportunity for Canadians to decide what is in their own interests — would be eroded by pressures for Canadian costs of production to match those in the United States. Pressures to render pensions, wage levels, unemployment insurance, tax, competition, regional development and even language policy (so fundamental to Canada's unity) identical with US ones would soon emerge. This is why the misgivings that Edward Blake put to Laurier in 1891 about "commercial union" with the United States remain valid today. "Assuming that absolute free trade with the States ... ought to come," Blake wrote, "I believe that it ... should only come as ... a well-understood precursor of political union ... Then so believing ... how can I properly recommend you now to decide upon commercial union?"

What are the alternatives for Canada if full "free trade" with the United States carries an unacceptably high price? "Global product mandating" (assigning international manufacture of a specific product or component to a Canadian plant) can frequently be found, on closer examination, to limit the factory's production, not broaden it. This is not to deny that efforts to achieve a product mandate by branch plants, even if limited to North America, are worth pursuing. But product mandating is no panacea. Research and development, local sourcing from specialist suppliers and, perhaps most important, entrepreneurial challenge will not generally flow from such mandating. In short, factories will not be turned into businesses by a product mandate alone. Additionally, if we do not first act to close our technological gap with the US (at least in certain industries), the benefits of bilateral free trade would flow to the place where innovation occurs: generally, the US headquarters.

The next Liberal government, in concert with business and labour, should instead concentrate on seeking a greater diversity of export markets for Canadian goods and services. It should provide additional incentives for domestic savers to invest in greater productive capacity. It should, preferably on a multilateral basis, negotiate the reduction or elimination of those non-tariff barriers currently hindering the entry of Canadian products into the US markets. Finally, it should promote, through investment, greater Canadian control of Canadian industry.

There are few things that Canadians make that potential foreign buyers cannot obtain elsewhere. So, the question of whether to "buy Canadian" frequently has more to do with the financial terms being offered than with the exact nature of the product. Our competitors have taken a lead in offering attractive financing. Their heavily subsidized interest rates have rightly been attacked as yet another form of beggar-thy-neighbour, with exporting countries competing among themselves to pay a subsidy to the importer. We could, of course, refrain from offering any such subsidized financing, but that would only give our competitors more reason to smile.

Half-hearted efforts have been made to agree on international limits for these subsidies. Although such efforts have been successful only occasionally, Canada should continue to support them. Pending international agreement, however, we shall achieve greater diversity in our export markets only when more attractive financial terms are offered. Liberal governments have increasingly given Canadian exporters the resources necessary to help make their bids more competitive. But the Export Development Corporation, the agency most concerned, is still limited in its ability to offer fully competitive terms. One of its goals has been to make an annual profit. That should be a secondary consideration, however, after promoting our exports more aggressively. To that end, the money made available to the EDC should be increased substantially.

Exports would also increase if there were greater investment by Canadians in their own country. With some exceptions, foreign-controlled subsidiaries have not been notably active in seeking additional export opportunities. If we owned more of our limited manufacturing industry, there would be long-term benefits in terms of our balance of payments. Canada would also supply both domestic and foreign markets with a greater range of specialized products.

One way to promote Canadian ownership and control is to tax investors in Canadian common stocks less on income from that source, at least within certain limits, or to permit the rollover of some investment without subjecting it to a capital gains tax. Admittedly, tax incentives (also called tax expenditures) reduce the taxes paid by some at the expense of others. But today's circumstances justify re-examining every method that encourages Canadians to move their savings out of banks and into shares of Canadian companies.

If we control more of our own industries, a more diversified, productive economy will result. The application of new technology to our existing industries, so vital to various regions, will also help. For example, our food exports have long been substantial, and the world's need for food continues to grow. In the past, however, exports have been largely raw food, not processed. Export-oriented innovation will lead to more investment in agriculture. The situation is similar in our mineral industries which, with intensive research, may find more efficient methods of exploiting lower grade ores, not to mention new applications for metals. Exploitation of our vast and diverse energy resources is obviously a motor for economic growth. But along with almost all other products from the Canadian cornucopia, energy developments will have limited impact unless we improve our transport system. The pressing need for rail and port improvements is, however, only one of the communications opportunities facing us. Whether in fibre optics, telecommunications or satellites, Canadian firms, large and small, have made promising beginnings. Now we must build on that base a more internationally competitive industry.

To do all these things, industry will need the assistance of governments, both national and provincial, to increase competitiveness and to help workers, even whole communities, adjust to changing competition. To be fully effective, however, two basic factors should also come into play.

First, we must reduce or eliminate the economic barriers which we have erected against ourselves within our own country. With the constitution and the Charter of Rights come improved opportunity to eliminate the remaining obstacles to the free flow of goods, services, investment capital and labour among all provinces.

Second, we need more consultation among business, governments and labour. Some call it "concertation," suggesting an orchestra, with each member playing his or her instrument but blending into a harmonious whole. The metaphor is a good one, since we cannot hope to contain inflation, achieve real growth, reduce unemployment or lessen regional disparities without all the participants following more or less the same score. The preparation of a report on business-government relations in 1976 underlined for me that only through more consultation of business, governments and labour canf we hope to reach the understanding, sector by industrial sector, necessary to increase research and development, acquire new capital equipment, provide tax incentives and grants, train workers for new technologies, and relate increases in earnings to increases in productivity. Also, both inflation and high technology bring social dislocation that can be contained only by broad co-operation, not by governments acting alone or management hoping inaction will somehow do the trick, or labour equating greater productivity and advanced technologies with lost jobs. Recently there has been some progress, but there remains a pressing need for additional places where business, government and organized labour can put their heads together. Unless we devise the machinery appropriate to our own circumstances, the economic problems will be even more difficult to overcome.

Such co-operation implies some degree of planning, some agreement freely entered into by all those most directly involved. If, for example, we conclude among ourselves that full employment can be achieved by means of the most internationally competitive industries, then those who can contribute will need to subscribe to joint action.

There is quite a history of such planning, both in terms of specific industries and in terms of government intervention in the economy.

Pearson wrote in 1962 that "the Liberal Party favours social and economic planning which will stimulate and encourage private enterprise to operate more effectively for the benefit of all." Six years later, John Turner elaborated:

> Liberalism must now accommodate itself to economic planning . . . I mean . . . an economy whose direction is charted by government with the advice and with the free co-operation of management, labour, farmers, and other economic groups so that long-term and short-term goals can be set for this country . . . it is a liberal response to changing conditions . . . Every business — large or small — plans, or should plan, for the future, and sets the target for itself. Surely, then, the largest and most important business of all, the business that concerns us most intimately, the government of Canada and her provinces, must plan. If government does not plan, no other business can.

But no plan, whether indicative or more detailed, is ever perfect. Each plan is obsolete before the ink is dry. What is required, then, are mechanisms to generate evolving industrial strategies on a continuing basis. This is a task for the party of reform.

The new constitution provides the framework for change and reform. While enshrining fundamental rights, its amending formula provides a means by which their protection may be increased. Co-operative federalism involves not only good will in federal-provincial negotiations but a ready means for allowing disputes to be adjusted through the constitutional amending process. Such co-operative federalism has a new opportunity to flourish. Each generation will, to a greater or lesser degree, re-order relations among regions and between Engish- and French-speaking Canadians in light of economic, technological and social change. But the framework that Liberals have devised will ensure that future adjustments will be within a constitution guaranteeing basic rights and freedoms to all.

Since the British conquest of New France, French-speaking Canadians have been understandably committed to ensuring the vitality of their culture (and hence their language) in an otherwise English-speaking North America. That vitality, which finds its fullest and most vigorous expression in Confederation, not the anxious vulnerability of a besieged minority, is now beyond question: a fact evident to all but the more myopic separatists.

A parallel concern has been political and later economic independence first from the British and more recently from the Americans. With the adoption of a new constitution, one hundred and fifteen years after Confederation, we took a major step in our ongoing political evolution. That is not, however, the end of our constitutional agenda. The Charter of Rights and Freedoms emphasizes sharing, but more remains to be done. The full realization of the benefits of our economic union, relations with the provinces and the territories, and added rights for all Canadians, including native peoples, will remain preoccupations of Liberals in Ottawa in decades ahead.

Additional problems, some not now foreseen, may hamper concerted action by Canadian governments, but among the manifold Liberal achievement, the new constitution is, in a sense, the crowning achievement. It offers the necessary means of reforming our most basic laws to our ever-changing needs. It answers a need that is part of the essence of liberalism, the need to seek, to strive and forever to begin anew.

Because the Liberal Party embraces a multiplicity of interests, it is also a kind of school. It is a good training ground for the art of governing, which is itself a process of harmonizing contending interests in such a way as to win the broad consent of those governed. This is a constant thread in Liberal history, and helps highlight the distinction between Liberals and Tories.

Given that their interest is more in the past and present than in the future, there is, in fact, an essential *dis*continuity in the policies of Conservatives. One is hard put to pinpoint those policies held in common by, say, Meighen, Diefenbaker and Clark. Certainly there is little there to give one any sense of regeneration. This is the very opposite of the attitude of Liberals who have instituted the social, economic, international and constitutional advances discussed in these pages.

Liberalism and conservatism were clearly born of different concepts of man. For the conservative, institutions and ideas sanctified and improved over generations are the surest guides to the future. They should be tampered with but seldom. If changed, they should be conserved in their essence. In the tradition of Edmund Burke, the conservative veneration of the past ascribes more wisdom to long-established institutions and practices than to the ability of men to improve them. "We are afraid," wrote Burke, "to put men to live and trade each an is small and that individuals would do better to avail themselves of the general bank and capital of nations and ages." Without the restraints imposed by society and adherence to precedent, man's fallen nature inclines him to rashness, error, inconsistency and unhappiness.

This description of the conservative makes it easy to understand why the Tories have so seldom held office in Ottawa. The mood of a new country, as Canada largely remains today, is not one of conservation but of construction; not of adherence to the past but of innovation for the future. The Liberal Party has been more in step with this mood, has been stimulated by it, and has done much in its turn to nurture it. Liberal leaders have been deeply sensitive to the plurality of Canada. Their practice of federalism has helped to ensure the regions great

104

autonomy within a unified country. There is nothing inevitable in this. The preservation of one Canada has been the most complex, and most unsung, task of Canadian governments. It has repeatedly called up all the powers of compromise, flexibility, creativity and innovationthat the Liberal Party has brought to federal politics over the years.

Liberalism has been suited to Canada in a yet deeper sense, too. For th willingness to give each person his or her opportunity, each culture the soil it needs to grow, is the essence of liberalism. Liberalism holds that when people act in freedom — free as far as possible from class or culture distinction and undue constraint — they may achieve not only self-fulfillment but the greatest public good. In this optimistic view, men in freedom are more prone to improve than to debauch themselves, more apt to perfect society and more likely, in the long run, to advance civilization.

Pressing forward in the 1980s and beyond will mean significant changes for liberalism, changes that will serve to dispel certain current generalities about its nature. Liberalism should not be equated with broad government internvention in the economy or expanding social policies, even though such programmes, aimed at giving scope to individual freedom and enterprise, remain essential. As the Liberal seeks to ensure opportunity, both in times of retrenchment as well as those economic growth, adapting such programmes will be his challenge.

"A state without the means of some changes is without the means of its conservation." In this instance, Burke was more liberal than conservative, and his words hold a compelling message. As Canadians confront the remainder of the twentieth century, they do so with new institutions better suited to their present needs and more adaptable to future ones.

BIBLIOGRAPHY

Butler, Rick and Jean-Guy Carrier, eds. *The Trudeau Decade.*
Toronto: Doubleday, 1979.

Cook, Ramsay. *Canada and the French-Canadian Question.*
Toronto: Macmillan, 1966.

Gwyn, Richard. *The Northern Magus: Pierre Trudeau and Canadians.*
Toronto: McClelland & Stewart, 1980.

Pearson, Lester B. *Words and Occasions.*
Toronto: University of Toronto Press, 1970.

——————— *Mike: The Memoirs of the Right Honourable
Lester B. Pearson.* 3 vols. Toronto: University of Toronto Press,
1972-75.

Pickersgill, J.W. *The Liberal Party.*
Toronto: McClelland & Stewart, 1962.

Radwanski, George. *Trudeau.* Toronto: Macmillan, 1978.

Shull, Joseph. *Laurier: The First Canadian.*
Toronto: Macmilland, 1965.

Trudeau, Pierre. *Federalism and the French Canadians.*
Toronto: Macmillan, 1968.

Turner, John N. *Politics of Purpose.*
Toronto: McClelland & Stewart, 1968.

Wearing, Joseph. *The L-Shaped Party.*
Toronto: McGraw-Hill Ryerson, 1981.

Whitaker, Reginald. *The Government Party.*
Toronto: University of Toronto Press, 1977.